Spirit Guides

Contact Your Spirit Guide and Access the Spirit World

(Learn How to Contact Your Spiritual Guides and Travel the Spiritual Plane Today)

Matthew Collins

Published By **Andrew Zen**

Matthew Collins

Spirit Guides: Contact Your Spirit Guide and Access the Spirit World (Learn How to Contact Your Spiritual Guides and Travel the Spiritual Plane Today)

ISBN   978-1-998901-43-2

Legal & Disclaimer

The information contained in this ebook is not designed to replace or take the place of any form of medicine or professional medical advice. The information in this ebook has been provided for educational & entertainment purposes only.

The information contained in this book has been compiled from sources deemed reliable, and it is accurate to the best of the Author's knowledge; however, the Author cannot guarantee its accuracy and validity and cannot be held liable for any errors or omissions. Changes are periodically made to this book. You must consult your doctor or get professional medical advice before using

Table Of Contents

Chapter 1: What is a Spirit Guide?

So the primary question that could arise whilst you're delving into this example, is what in the international a spirit guide is. A spirit guide isn't only a few little entity, but as an opportunity, there is a lot that you can discover about this, and there are a number of cool elements to this that you can not even comprehend as well. A spirit manual is truely an interesting situation rely for plenty people, because it's some thing that you can use to enhance yourself, however this economic catastrophe will float over first and fundamental what it's miles, and some statistics approximately the person of it.

Have you ever heard of a so-known as "dad or mum angel" this is famous inside the Christian religion? According to the religion, the ones guardians exist for humans, watch over them, and are seen as a shape of defensive entity that is going through lifestyles. Well, in a feel, a spirit manual is much like this. However, this is more of an man or woman spirit in a feel, and it's seen specifically inside the Native American, Chinese, or perhaps in Egyptian information.

These are seen as a shape of ancient being that you may look to and are looking for advice from. Often, a number of the famous sorts of spirit guides that people do partner with are saints, beatified people, or maybe nature spirits, however in this case, we're going to move over what in full-size a spirit manual is.

Now, consistent with most humans, a spirit manual is an energy on a cosmic degree, or perhaps a slight entity, this is considered a very effective spirit manual. They're no longer continuously taken into consideration human, but they do from time to time have human lives that they relate to. In some instances, the ones publications may additionally have a past lifestyles, some shape of karmic nature to it or a debt that they've to pay, or they're past the area of being able to change or reincarnate into every distinct shape. For many individuals who bear in mind in spirit courses, they aren't decided on with the resource of humans however as an alternative thru the alternative thing, that's the arena after lack of existence. These courses are taken into consideration important because they are capable of provide assist to particular humans.

Some spiritualist don't without a doubt recollect that the ones courses aren't that important, due to the truth the ones spirit courses are visible as lessening electricity and it would furthermore be considered a form of disrespect to humans. However, most people who use the ones do get helped with the useful resource of the spirit, but typically they're now not visible as appointed to help the individual however rather they'll be round and people can visit for assist once they want it.

Many times notwithstanding the truth that, people see the ones spirit guides as entities that have been assigned to us in advance than we have been even born, which means that this spirit manual is taken into consideration a completely crucial part of your existence. Think of those publications as a shape of nudge tool for masses folks. They form of supply us the rush that we want in lifestyles, and that would truly be useful with many those who are trying to beautify their lives. According to many, those guides have a shape of agreement that they want us to satisfy on this earth, and we make this agreement and try and fulfill it in advance than we pass on and get reincarnated into a few thing else. Think of the spirit manual as a mentor, and your higher self virtually will assist us get the proper guide that we need in existence, in order that we're able to have the fine and maximum a achievement incarnation that we can live out.

Now, the element approximately those guides is there are kinds. There's one, kind of similar to the little pal that you paintings to consult who sticks around. Many instances, this may be visible because of the reality the angel for your shoulder who insists that you bypass inside the path of the proper problem. This kind of spirt manual doesn't leave, however alternatively they stay with you in the course of your entire lifestyles as a form of secondary character to transport inside the route of. There are however, extraordinary spirit courses that don't do this, however as an alternative they arrive by means of once in a while to help you out. These styles of spirit courses are generally greater powerful than the each day one, and they're alleged to help with a high quality a part of an area that you're suffering with, or perhaps a intention which you're strolling to gain.

Now, the spirit guides furthermore have incredible stages of being aware, as you may begin to see. Some of them are past masters (for example Jesus or maybe Buddha), and others can also seem greater like your average run-of-the-mill spirit that may be a grasp of 1 vicinity, which embody perhaps a spirit guide for song or perhaps sports. They might also additionally have a male strength or even a girl electricity in a revel in, but at the bottom of it it's actually really power in favored. They don't honestly associate with a gender. You may also moreover have a spirit that appears extra bodily than a few other, inclusive of even being in the form of someone or animal, however from time to time, they could certainly look greater like an ethereal energy that doesn't appear like a body in any respect.

For a number of the ones spirit courses, they might be guiding a couple of character, or they might be first-rate running with you, so keep that during thoughts. Most of the time those spirits aren't associated with you or in reality each person you apprehend, however as an alternative they're spirits that have been assigned that will help you.

What the ones spirit guides do is pretty easy. When the time is proper, they'll pass right into the electricity which you personal, and that they paintings to change it into the satisfactory form, and they artwork that will help you satisfy the undertaking which you have accessible. It's pretty exquisite once you start to see what you may do after you song into the spirit guide which you have in existence.

That is what the general description of a spirit guide is. They do an entire lot as well, and inside the next financial ruin, we'll delve into in addition element and discern out just what precisely these spirit guides can completely do for you.

Chapter 2: What a Spirit Guide Can do for You

Now that you realize what a spirit manual is, it's time to head over surely what the ones courses can do for you. They have a whole variety of skills and powers that they own, however they seem them in sure methods. You may not even realise that the spirit manual is assisting you on the onset until you seek advice from and clearly test it, however the truth is, you can reap those spirit guides that will help you beautify your existence, and this economic catastrophe will pass into similarly element approximately how the ones spirit courses assist manual you and artwork to interfere to improve and attain what you want to in existence.

The first detail that they may do is ship you signs and signs and symptoms and signs and symptoms and signs and symptoms. These courses can alternate topics and help you spot some aspect which you need to recognize about. They can synchronize fine events that will help you, and also you need to be careful for while the ones takes region. Think about it, you won't comprehend it initially, but then if you start to have a observe lifer, you will see that it's the spirit guide. Have you ever had three similar events take location at the identical time? Maybe you're thinking about what to consume, and then you definitely see three unique signs and signs and symptoms for a hen salad. That's now not just a twist of destiny after a while, because of the truth you will probable see all of them internal a small span of time. That's a spirit guide, and also you want to be aware of it, get the message, and circulate from there.

Also, spirit publications can help with the intestine feelings which you could have. You could in all likelihood every now and then feel a few issue interior you. Often, this is how a spirit guide communicates to you, and also you want to be privy to it when it occurs for the duration of superb stories. That is a manner to speak to you that you need to pay attention to what's occurring. Maybe you've felt this way in advance than, but if you've ever had that everyday, bizarre feeling that a few factor virtually lousy is ready to take place however you may't completely determine it out, that's usually the spirt guide telling you deep down that that may be a few element that you want to be aware of, and it's for your exceptional interest to do sincerely that.

Then there may be the intuition that you building up over the years. You might also experience a small alternate in your instinct that might be telling you to both sluggish down, boost up, or perhaps truely not pass for a few trouble. You may moreover get the thoughts that some thing terrible is happening in conjunction with your dating, in any other case you want to bypass check on your cat. These flashes and changes may additionally seem right away, however often, they do provide a outstanding clue to what's taking location for your universe. It is some thing that you should be aware of, that's for certain. Many won't take note of what their instinct has to say half of the time, but often, there is information to behold in case you make an effort and be aware of this.

Then there may be the situation of having sure our our bodies collectively that lets in you to create a meeting that changes matters. This is a common detail that your spirit manual makes use of a amazing way to get a meeting among human beings to change matters. Let's take for instance which you're considering you amazing friend you haven't talked to in all of the time, and then abruptly they text you out of nowhere. Maybe you have got been considering that one man which you located at the fitness center, and then they display up out of nowhere at the community coffee preserve. You may also first count on that this is all simplest a chance encounter, or a twist of fate which you shouldn't placed an lousy lot idea into, however that's in that you're incorrect. You can be considering moving somewhere, and then you definitely honestly run proper right into a realtor that you worked with inside the beyond, and every now and then despite the fact that that doesn't look like a few issue greater than a twist of fate, it is able to be the spirit guide in search of to get you together for a purpose. It can also even play matchmaker in great situations, so it's of significance to art work with this and notice it for what it's miles.

Then there can be the fact that they're capable of nudge you and push you in the proper route, even without that means to doing so. For example, allow's say you out of area your pockets and you may't discover it. You're developing aggravated, and then all of a surprising, your cellular smartphone rings. You take it, and it's the business enterprise call which you've been waiting for and that candy vending that you've coveted for goodbye. Now, you'll possibly simply assume that it come to be a twist of destiny, and then fast once you magically discover your keys, indicating that maybe you have been clearly searching over them or some aspect. A lot of people who've this occur to them often simply brush aside the signs as some element that happens, however the fact is, if you have a look at it, you'll probable comprehend that the spirit guide tried to cover your wallet so you may additionally moreover need to make the effort to take that call, because of the reality in any other case even as you're inside the vehicle and using you cannot take it. Now, you may begin to realize this after some time at the same time as you search for the clues that they gave you, and regardless of the reality that it is able to be frustrating like no distinctive due to what they do, it's on your amazing pursuits to surrender the manipulate to them and permit them to have their fun, because of the truth most of the time, they've got some component large coming down the runway, so that you want to take it gradual and art work with the spirit, no matter the fact that it is able to be worrying.

They also can assist you enhance your capacity to certainly assist with your existence. If you're growing a large preference collectively with your place of work on whether or no longer to move for the contemporary day technique, you could all at once see a sign that basically tells you it's a excellent difficulty to do it, or possibly you get a danger call while you're looking at a few factor regarding the selling and you listen simply how proper it's far. Perhaps you begin to see the beauty of the advertising and marketing, and these signs and symptoms actually maintain on popping up. If that's the case, it may not honestly be a threat come upon, however as an alternative, it's some element that you ought to consider while you're searching for to have a splendid existence. These spirit publications do seem themselves in small techniques, and they will be capable of sincerely assist you.

Your spirit guide can do a lot for you, and that they permit you to gain the goals that you need. Think approximately it this manner: they will be just like the little voice to your head which you pay interest every so often, and it might be visible as a kind of sense of proper and wrong, however the reality is, it's in fact some thing that you need to keep in mind, pay attention to, and paintings to decorate your communications with this spirit manual, because of the fact it can really assist you.

Chapter 3: How to Directly Connect to Spirit Guides

Now, this monetary break will pass over and assist you right now connect with the spirit manual that you want. Now, there are clean things that you could do a good way to be referred to inside the next financial ruin, but if you're seeking out immediate symptoms and outcomes, with an instantaneous connection that works outstanding and without any stops, then this is for you. Now, it might be incredible if you can clearly press a button to your cell phone and from the app the spirit manual proper now tells you what to do, the destiny you can own, and what you need to get proper away. It might be top notch to have that, however for optimum it's tough to accumulate that. Now, you might be capable of help decorate your spirit manual connection, in order that you may be stated as properly in some time, but it does take some time. Here are a few methods to proper now connect to out too much problem, so you can do the ones and ten running on honing this as properly.

The first is to pay attention to the instinct that you have. Now, this is much less complicated said than performed, due to the fact most humans generally tend to ignore their instinct most of the time, however that's not quite the way it really works. It's no longer the manner you're going to get effects in existence, and you received't hook up with the spirit manual, and as a substitute it's going to handiest make the relationship worse. What you need to but start to do is to concentrate to the ones gut emotions and also you need to make sure which you're taking note of it efficaciously. If it says you need to visit the health club in preference to run outdoor these days, do that, because you will likely hold yourself from an ugly fall that you might in all likelihood otherwise have. If you however, pay interest some thing which embody "you'll in no manner make it, you're honestly unpleasant," then don't be aware about that. The ego can be virtually tough with this, due to the fact it can every so often permit you to apprehend which you're now not correct enough, in any other case you're too right, and that could trade the manner your feelings are. However, if you are listening to moves in place of emotions in terms of what your instincts are telling you, then it's to your first-rate hobby to listen to that intuition, because you'll connect to your spirit as nicely.

You need to moreover be privy to the intestine intuition that you have. Your intestine is one way to direct you. For example, permit's say that you're paying attention to a possible business organisation deal in a meeting, and your gut says to now not comply with it, due to the truth they gained't help you, and also you'll emerge as having to choose up the portions. Or maybe you're on a date with a cutting-edge-day man, and it's telling you that the brilliant detail to do is to live pals, and that's the intestine feeling. Or possibly, you get the intestine feeling that your cat desires to see the vet or some aspect. Listen to it. If it doesn't experience proper in a nice state of affairs, together with possibly you're out with someone or jogging on a mission. The odds are, that if it's not a few issue you enjoy accurate and fantastic approximately, it's now not going to stop quite. You ought to use the gut emotions to shield something you need to guard, and from there, you could help be a part of and make stronger the bond in conjunction with your spirit manual.

Then there may be the looking out for signs and symptoms. You ought to search for the precise signs and symptoms which is probably to be had. You won't comprehend this, however there are symptoms that come approximately in uncommon techniques. You might not also be information of those symptoms in advance than the whole thing, however they will be there. They are available in wonderful office work, and you won't understand it until you think about it. Perhaps you're looking to eat wholesome and also you want a few factor for dinner however don't recognise what to have. You magically see a billboard signal for this dish that's low in electricity but excessive in all the good things you need. You then make it, and you feel specific. That's a signal, and also you might not even comprehend it. Perhaps as nicely that in all likelihood you have got got been thinking about a salad and your spouse or friend brings you one for dinner. Yes, that could start to be some detail that you don't comprehend, however over time, they typically are available threes. So, if a few element occurs 3 instances, it's on your exceptional pastimes to be privy to this, because of the truth it may in reality help you.

Then there can be the magazine. Having a mag is a exquisite way to connect to your spirit guide. You want to open it, or maybe simply use a phrase record to help with this, and then write down whatever questions you experience your spirit guide can answer. Just wait, and be meditative approximately the solutions that stand up. Keep going, and feel such as you're having a verbal exchange with them. This also can initially sense which incorporates you're clearly making things up, however you want to hold going, and every so often, you may get to the extent in which the voices which you are listening to aren't those that sound together with you. Notice that, after which start to hold on, due to the fact this can help.

Then, there may be dreaming. This is a first rate way to hook up with sure guides and then be part of up. You can open up, and then dream approximately them. Eventually, this will work, and on occasion you can connect with them for your goals. These publications might in all likelihood take a piece to waltz proper in, but they'll come, and from time to time if you're a lucid dreamer, this can be even better, because of the reality then they may talk to you.

Finally, there can be asking a psychic. These human beings do offer readings and help for oldsters which might be interested in their spirit courses. This is a terrific way that will help you in case you're now not certainly getting the solutions that they want, and from time to time those psychics will let you get pointed inside the proper direction. It's a fantastic manner to help you with this, and also you'll revel in better as properly.

Now, your final element that you must recognize about whilst you're trying to connect with your spirit guide is help inside the question of in case you're just imagining this, of if it's real. This is a commonplace issue with many, because of the truth they frequently enjoy like they're simply imagining the subjects which can be springing up, but there are some symptoms which you need to take into account. The first is that if it resonates with you. Something this is made up in your mind will no longer resonate with you deeply. However, you may be conscious it straight away if it sticks spherical and resonates very deeply into your coronary coronary heart, and for your mind.

Then there may be if you feel locate it impossible to resist's coming from a person else besides you. If it feels in comparison for your voice, then it's almost truely a spirit guide coming. Then there can be the advice, and if it makes revel in to you. If it does seem proper, and now not some thing that you make up, then greater than likely it's valid. You want to moreover look to look if you're getting results from this. Hear them more than one times, and if you do what they may be saying and it even though works, then via all way, it's in fact a spirit guide nicely well worth taking note of. They moreover paintings to seem on the equal time and in the same form, and if that's the case, you may extra than probable be seeing a spirit guide. You should be searching out for those solutions, for they'll assist you.

Chapter 4: Little Things to assist Strengthen Your Spirit Guide Power

Now, you do realise the way to invite the spirit publications for immediate help, however there are some matters that you may do at the same time as you do are looking for advice from and get recommendation, and people are essential. If you're now not really getting effects with the recommendations in advance, then begin to use those that will help you. These allow you to decorate and boom the relationship that you so preference to have together collectively together with your sprite manual nearly proper now, and it does an entire lot.

The first is to invite surely. Often, they may be top with unique and easy goals and techniques to assist. They can help with the whole lot from supporting you find out a pinnacle parking region to even supporting with getting higher from grief or unhappiness. You also may be able to assist meet your destiny lifestyles companion as well, and it let you get thru an entire lot. In this, the requests are limitless regardless of how huge or hoe minuscule they may be, however you need to ask and ask in reality.

Don't have a fuzzy aim in hand, because of the reality normally, if that's the case, they have got problem with answering the message.

Then there can be the truth that you want to be unattached to what's going to reveal up and now not be too emotionally effected through it. For many folks that start off, they wait patiently like a dog watching for meals for the spirit guide to go back again again, and they preferred them to be immoderate and deliver the answers proper away. Many human beings do need them to experience like a friend or family member, and that they need to recognize the data as properly. They every so often don't forget these spirit guides as a top notch friend who will pop over for a few drinks, however you want to do away with that attitude immediately. The reason for this is due to the fact they don't typically come out that manner. You moreover shouldn't be connected to what they are announcing, but instead open up your mind for the possibilities. Your spirit guide is your friend, however usually you could't really dictate what shape of person and the very last outcomes with them. They would probably seem like the type of character that you could exit and feature beverages with, but they're now not that. They're purported to be guiding you, no longer guiding you to glad hour.

Then there is the spirit steerage difficulty that you can put into effect into your life. This is a completely small issue, however it may in reality help you with connecting and getting the answers which you need. You must get a small area that is unique and you've some connection to, and then have that field due to the fact the delineated spirit manual subject. On it, you should then write a question on some paper, or perhaps some thing unique which you want assist with. Once you do that, you then fold up the paper and ten located it within the field. This is a manner for the spirit guide to head returned right in and offer you with the assist which you want, although it's a piece more difficult at the way to get the overall sign which you need.

Speaking of symptoms and symptoms and signs and symptoms, asking for a signal is simply one of the great strategies to help get a better connection to your spirit guide. A sign is truely a way to definitely get the direct answer which you choice. To do that, you need to get a particular object that may be a manner to collect the communication from the guide, or perhaps the way you need to deliver it out. It can be some thing which you need to use, which consist of a feather, an ornament, a superstar, or maybe vegetation. You ought to have this nearby, leave it for the spirit guide, and you may then get a sign from them. This is a manner to leave little symptoms which you want to have, and that is a manner to get a direct communique from the spirit manual while you so want it.

Then there is growing a place that is taken into consideration sacred and a place that lets in you to proper away hook up with the spirit guide. This is similar to the shrines which you could see in rooms in sure cultures, however that is a extraordinary manner to genuinely get communications from the manual. To do this, select out a niche, which include possibly the window ledge, the nightstand nearby, or maybe a touch board in which you have got high quality photos or something. This may be like this kind of foam boards you notice in a more youthful female's room. Now, what you do is then you definitely spend a hint little little bit of time every day to connect to the guides. You can meditate and ask them for assist, or perhaps tape or place the query or piece of recommendation that you want help with up. You need to spend about ten minutes each day doing this, due to the fact making an funding time into the spirit will permit you to have a higher dating with the spirits.

Then there can be intuitive writing, or writing in a deep way. This is much like the magazine defined earlier than, however you want to have the communications with them, and do that with unique coloured pens. Have the gap be sacred as nicely via lighting fixtures a candle or maybe burning incense. Once you do this, you could then spend a while truly writing down the severa questions and thoughts that you have, and appearance ahead to the spirits to answer you and provide you with the recommendation that you need.

Now, allow's say that you're strolling on a particular process or a few issue and also you need a few assist, you can even get the terrific spirit guides obtainable. Let's say that you are trying to art work for your very last essay on your semester in college and it's huge, and also you're having lots of hassle with it. If you're having a tough time with it, you may have a instructor or a scholar guide to help you with something conditions that you have reachable. Call for the ones that will help you, and you could truly have them be a bit precise, such as possibly the smart antique man for philosophy, or the fashionista manual for something associated with style. You may not consider it straight away, however there are publications for every shape of little factor available, so it's in your first-rate interest to call at the extremely good, or the ones which is probably fitting to the hobby on hand. You will not keep in mind it first of all, however it simply does paintings.

You have to additionally ensure now not to micromanage them, due to the truth that's not how they artwork. Just like with maximum matters in life, the extremely good leaders may be folks who clever approximately the mission, after which accept as actual with the others to get the activity which you need finished. Think of your self because the chief and the courses are the humans. You shouldn't need to micromanage and make certain that they're doing the whole thing, due to the reality 9 instances out of ten they will be running on it. You have to be smooth approximately what you want and what you need them to do, after which, you need to very well don't forget them at the venture and assume that they'll get it performed. You shouldn't have any bad emotions or doubts approximately their ability. Remember, some of those guides are definitely very effective entities, and in case you name at the excellent personnel, you will get the hobby finished, so they'll have the ability to help you.

You also can hold a document of the severa desires, visions, or perhaps any guidance and intuitive feelings that you get. Maybe in some unspecified time in the future you see a signal three times and take a look at up in your cat or a few element like that. You won't apprehend them inside the beginning, but in case you allow the ones signs begin to be ascribed to your magazine, you may begin to see it. You can also have the ones accessible as nicely as a way to see a sample. Maybe this is the way you delineate what your spirit manual will seem like or some thing of the type. It's pretty magical as quickly as you work on this, due to the fact this will will allow you to get the steering which you want, and assist you to consider the spirit guides while you need to. If you're writing subjects down, you may then have an real file of this, and you may be able to touch items and problems which can be often seen as intangible forces.

Finally, you may additionally use your wants to help connect. This is just like what became stated within the final bankruptcy, but that is taken to every exclusive diploma. The first issue is, in advance than you go to bed you want to mentally ask on your spirit courses to come returned to you to your goals. When you wake up, the primary trouble which you do is hold close the journal in which you hold your recordings and then write down the whole thing that you hold in thoughts which you acquired in your goals, which encompass the messages you bought. Now, you may not have a conscious memory of it, but no matter all of that, you have to virtually write down the information this is coming to you in the mag. You need to positioned down the whole thing that looks and is derived to mind, despite the fact that it sounds loopy and makes no experience. It might be the manner you communicate to your spirit manual although it seems sincerely bizarre.

All of these are severa methods that will help you decorate the conversation amongst you and your spirit manual. This is the set of techniques that you can use that will help you get a proper away, real answer if you're seeking out some thing of that type. Now, it's miles splendid in case you take the ones into interest while you figure on this, due to the fact you'll be able to have a far higher life, and a far higher result in case you reflect onconsideration on all of this, and you figure on enhancing your communications with the spirits so you can apprehend them greater.

Chapter 5: Meditations to Help with Your Spirit Guide

Now, you could use all of those to help with enhancing your verbal exchange together together together with your spirit guide, but there can be a incredible medium that you can use to connect to the spirit guide that you desire. That is thru meditation, and this financial ruin will move into details of why you may use meditation, and a couple of clean meditations to assist/.

The first meditation that may be beneficial is the subsequent: what you want to do is to picture yourself going right right into a room, after which asking simply in your publications to move again to you so that you can sit down down with them and speak. You want to then have a magazine close by, and once anybody is there, write down what they're saying. At first, this is probably fuzzy, however if the relationship will become more potent over the years, the statistics can be clearer, and you can have a better manner to apply it in your lifestyles.

There is also this mediation that you can use to help you with this, and it's essential to be aware this. To start, you need to have a quiet space that's actual for you which ones may be furthermore cushty, and additionally an area that isn't full of out of doors distractions. Often, some people pays interest extra with tune, so has that there, and you can also have a sacred item within the front of you, along facet a candle, or perhaps a few incense. Once you've got were given that, it's time to lighten up the body via inhaling thru your nose and out via your mouth. Feel your energy open up, and enjoy your self turn out to be extra open to this. Once you do that, you can additionally carry out a hint stretching, feeling the manner your body has the small pulls and sinews, and it may be a excellent way that will help you in reality lighten up yourself. Once you do this, then you definitely definately close to your eyes and characteristic your attention be focused inward on yourself.

Then, there can be the contact country of this, in that you've were given were given your non secular reason intact and available so you can talk on your manual. You can at this component do a prayer for religious guide to assist with enhancing touch, and you may try this when you touch your guide.

When you call the cut up guide, you obtain this inwardly. This is all subjective, so it's what you are making of it. You need to begin to end up extra aware of the truth that they're there. In usually, you would possibly see them, enjoy them, pay attention them, and you may necessarily understand that they're there. You could be there as nicely, and the satisfactory detail to do is to sit down there, and inform them "suited day" as a manner to connect to them. Then, wait a piece bit for them to receive your communique, and then have them can help you recognise right day again.

When you do this, you want to breathe, smooth your thoughts, and genuinely be there. You need to do this without talking, and as quick as the whole thing is cleared ask them within the occasion that they have got a message for you. Once you try this, sit down spherical and pay attention to the religious conversation, and be open for it. You want to be absolutely nonetheless for this and open to receiving it, even though it might be difficult at times.

After a few minutes, or when you revel in discover it impossible to resist's right, you want to then take your palms and located them within the the the front of your coronary heart, retaining them there. You need to then inform them "thank you" to the spirit guide, and you can pass into a bigger thank you for everything that they do in lifestyles. You have to then begin to drift some distance from focusing at the spirit manual, and then interest on your self.

At this point, you have to start to notice the way you sense after you've finished up the meditation and the manner your body is. You could probable immediately have a look at the modifications, or it would take you a couple of minutes to do that. Once completed, you have to then take some breaths to assist floor you and convey you decrease lower back to truth, and then, it's time to open up your eyes.

Now, it might appear like a loopy detail doing this, and for a 2d, you will likely start to surprise what to do about this. What you should do is deliver your self a bit of time to machine the whole lot that came about in advance than you preserve on collectively along side your day. In all honesty, typically the those who begin to get those symptoms and signs and symptoms and signs and symptoms from their meditation would possibly seem a piece pressured with the useful resource of all of this. However, in case you take some time to examine what they stated, check how that session can help you, and discover ways to make out simply what this all way, the entirety receives higher. Do that, and you then'll be able to have a higher focus on existence. You also can seek advice from the magazine that you need to put in writing down the experience, walk for a piece bit, or maybe meditate for a chunk and take the enjoy that you had and look at your self, feeling what you want to enjoy from this. This will come up with a few extra time and some endurance, and from there, you'll enjoy even higher as nicely.

These are some of the great equipment that you may use an excellent way to assist with meditation. By the usage of meditation to assist with this, you'll be capable of decorate the pleasant of your existence, the way the whole lot is, or even the recognition of what you're like now. It's a manner to help you decorate the manner your life is, and it's a way to take the whole lot that you've determined from the spirit manual that you have, after which you may virtually approach the statistics that you have that allows you to enhance and take your existence to the subsequent degree that you want it to.

Chapter 6: Unveiling the Spiritual World

Since the start of the human race, the populace of this universe have been uncountable. The facts and the beginning of the human race are even though many of the maximum interest looking for and mysterious questions, for all. This hobby has also induced a number of precise myths referring to the ones troubles. But all this curiosity and series of myths is prepared the bodily being of human beings, which has the great possibilities to be supported through clues and seen precedence. The bodily presence may be decided and noticed, however there may be another wider and greater complicated attitude of human life, this is the non secular worldwide.

The international of spirits is whole of controversies and a couple of critiques. But those types of accept as true with manual the complex patterns of this global.

The international of Spirits is the arena wherein the spirits live. Although considered to be separated from the natural physical global, the religious global is in constant interplay with the herbal worldwide. But this interplay is invisible or unnoticeable with the aid of manner of the bigger masses.

This explanation is the maximum easy one, for the beginners who are within the direction in their manner of statistics the truth of spiritual international.

The non secular bodies or the spirits:

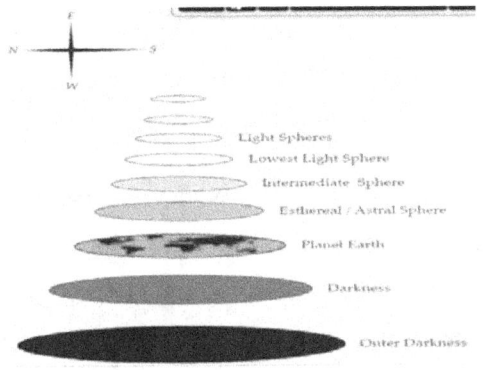

The worldwide of spirits is having more than one spirits, all of which very personal extra younger look. There is not any idea of the antique age inside the global of spirits. Many human beings question about the spirits of antique age human beings or Children and babies getting into the religious global. In that area the time span to broaden to maturity passes thru in a miles shorter time. Spiritual maturity may be discerned inside the countenance and light of a spiritual body. The spirits can enlarge or settlement but not just like the physical worldwide it's miles determined thru the usage of the quantity or sphere of the sector, which a spirit possesses. The attainment of the maximum length is likewise ruled with the resource of a specific degree wherein the spirit is residing.

When spirit movements from the natural global to the non secular worldwide the physical and the spiritual presence may additionally furthermore variety. As one in every of a kind spheres of religious international location travelled through the usage of way of a selected body, it is able to alternate the arrival, which may additionally moreover range from its physical appearance of the herbal worldwide. The number one elements of this appearance which may additionally moreover moreover variety encompass the height and period. Moreover, the spirits emanate a particular energy or radiance. The nature and quantity of this radiance is likewise determined by way of manner of a particular sphere of the spiritual international.

Some elements of the sector of spirits:

The factors of spirits at the way to be noted on this phase will seem quite simple to 3 humans. But those are the most queries which come within the mind of people who want to understand approximately the worlds of spirits and invisible entities.

The invisible spheres during the earth

? Clothing

As against the seen clothes possessed thru using the character in the herbal international, the non secular our our bodies possess a selected "air of thriller", it honestly is synonymous to the garments for the spirits. The spirits of the bottom sphere seem with their naked our bodies and because the tour in the course of the only of a kind tiers, the air of mystery receives brighter and brighter. Right after the shortage of existence, the physical effect of the frame dominates, however as the spirits advantage manipulate over the spiritual forces at their disposal, the aura gets extra willing toward the non secular look. The coloration range within the spiritual global is past the earthly combination of seven simple rainbow sunglasses. The type of hues and the sun sun shades of colors within the spiritual worldwide visit lots.

Clothing this is pertinent inside the spiritual sphere, has sunglasses and textures taken from the splendid of the non secular scenario of the spirit. Each exacting sphere has its individual and one in every of a type tone of coloration steady with the interests, religious intensity, gifting or perception and acquaintance of its populace.

? Language

In the spiritual realm the communique is made feasible via thoughts and impressions. The verbal language of earthly beginning isn't normal inside the religious international. In the spiritual worldwide the verbal exchange is at a complicated degree of understanding and communicating, in which the in depth understanding is made viable through the deep thoughts of the spirits. The textual content and written manuscript are quality required in our earthly communique. The spirits are past this need. Many of the philosophers who have completed deep assessment at the spiritual international kingdom that if a spirit wants to recognize a few entity in the non secular global, the spiritual area lets in the spirit to grow to be that entity and experience it to the intensity absolutely. This ability "to grow to be, what you want to apprehend" is through the combination of notion and subjective understanding.

? Sight

The sight in the non secular international is one-of-a-type for the spirits, which reason them to invisible for all of the earthly creatures. Because of the contrasting nature of attractions, not handiest the spirits are out of the sight of the earthly creatures, but for the spirits furthermore, the earth and its population appear to be a mist or hue. But for the spirits residing in the decrease tiers of the spiritual global, the sight may be just like the earthly populace as they are at the lower realm. Some spirits, regardless of being inside the non secular international may also undergo religious blindness, which makes them blind in the direction of the aura and hue of the top tiers of the non secular global.

? Memory

When a spirit leaves the bodily frame, the instances and the happenings of the soul, in the direction of the earthly lifestyles, are saved inside the thoughts of the soul. The mind possessed through manner of the bodily body is handiest a sensation for the spirit. These sensations additionally derive the human life. In the earthly existence, the spirit and the bodily life may not be in harmony, due to the fact the sensations of the spirit and the sensations of the body may be in evaluation. The depth of memory is greater in religious global, wherein pain, happiness, satisfaction and pride are felt and professional with a exceptional deal greater depth and saved as a eternal affect.

Chapter 7: Actions and sports sports inside the religious worlds

For the earthy life the attainment of a financially robust existence with all of the elements of survival, denotes a rich lifestyles. In the bodily international, the physical desires of meals, secure haven and belongingness govern the complete lifestyles struggle of the human beings. But the non secular realm is beyond those intention dimensions of survival. It is a place in which the physical needs bring no region, alternatively the inner self and the deep attainment of glory is needed.

? Spiritual global lets in without delay notion:

During our worldly direction of life, all the time we're struggling to take some proper preference. From the smallest household chores to the most vital and broader perspectives of corporation lifestyles, our actions are driven with the resource of our alternatives. In the choice making the opportunity of fulfillment or getting the favorable final results isn't always hundred percentage. It is because of the reality the ability to take the proper choice is bounds with the resource of our physical senses. However, in the non secular global, the spirits are granted with the higher degree of notion and information. Because of this superiority of spirits, people try to speak with their spirit guides as a manner to get help from the higher degree of perception of the spirits. Some preference or ambiguity it truly is past the information of the human knowledge can without issues be interpreted with the aid of the use of the use of the spirits. So if an individual is underneath the steerage of the spirits, he or she will be capable of make a rational or favorable selection. The belief of the spirits is despite the fact that superior to the people.

? The "notion" governs the "sight"

In the non secular realm the bodily want and desires are quite precise from the humanly dreams. Here in the global, we are able to see handiest what's inside the the front of our eyes. If a few component isn't visible we can be capable of make some imagination or notion approximately that entity, however this belief varies from character to individual. For the spirits the better degree of perception is the maximum powerful tool. For people, we may additionally furthermore say that "seeing is believing", but for spirits belief is more critical. The higher degree of insight possessed with the resource of the spirits makes them higher in desire making compared to humans, which calls for the want of spirit manual. Sometimes whilst you connect with your sprit guide, you revel in a unethical to behave in a particular way. After you act for that reason, you stumble upon the consequences and take delivery of as proper with that it'd had been contrary in outcomes, if you act parallel in your guide. This concludes that for the spirits the insight superimposes the physical sight, possessed via the humans.

? Thoughts and emotions are unveiled

The physical existence has been designed in this form of way that some of things in the internal self of the character are hidden for others to see or take a look at. The feeling of hatred and jealousy are generally hidden till installed thru movements. In the non secular realm the inner self of every spirit is unveiled. On the label of this purity and piety the suitable spheres of the spiritual worldwide are resided through truely one in every of a type spirits. Once the readability of the internal self is carried out, the spirit is moved to the pinnacle sphere.

Chapter 8: Mystic Mysteries

The moves and sports activities within the global of spirits have contrasting dimensions, in assessment to the bodily worldwide. For the earthly creatures and the population of this planet, the arena of spirits, seem as "airy fairy", that's beyond the bodily size of objectivity. Likewise, within the international of spirits, the earthly life isn't a robust life. The exceptional existent and unyielding subjects and entities within the spiritual international are those composed of "spiritual essence." The bodily existence of human beings and wonderful living beings on the planet seem to the spirits as "vapor". The entire aim international in the world looks like a "mist" that is touchy and close to to be blown away.

Not satisfactory the human beings and different creatures seem as a hue and mist, however all of the bodily property and property are meaningless for the spirits dwelling in specific spheres of spirituality. From the spiritual mind-set, the factor of distinction isn't the maintaining of any position or acquiring some asset, rather for the non secular region, fulfillment is accounted for, in terms of kindness, gratitude and being useful. The religious spheres are divided into one-of-a-type spheres, wherein each better sphere contains of spirits who are better in assisting others, and striving for the collective welfare. This present physical global makes a speciality of intellectual attainment and outward consequences, however inside the spiritual global, spirits awareness at the internal purpose and foundation of the results.

? The Mystery of Creation and Observance of the Spiritual worldwide:

For the humans the capacity to appearance or perhaps revel in the non secular international is quite confined. It calls for non-save you efforts and a alternate in the life-style and the thinking method. The physical frame and the thoughts of people can also get a glimpse of the spiritual realities, however the full fledge acquisition of the religious knowledge is beyond the human mind.

One of the finest variations the various spiritual worldwide and the physical international is the related domain names of time, region and strength. For the earth and its inhabitants the lifestyles denotes a selected time, area and power, however for the spirits, the existing location is past the regulations of place time and energy. To recognize this difference, someone desires to craft out the difference of physical time, it is linear in evaluation to religious time, that could adjust, relying upon the dominion of mind of the spirit. Similarly the bodily place being linear is denoted through distance, even as the spiritual place is extra like a mental place for the spirit.

The spirits studies time via specific sports, region via mind and electricity through the spiritual life pulsating from the coronary heart. It can also additionally rise up that a non secular experience may also moreover ultimate best for one earth second, but be like one week, for the spirit. On earth the human beings experience linear time via atoms and the movement of the earth across the sun, but the Spiritual time may be lengthened or shortened and it attains its pulsed existence shape the spirits.

The first-rate spheres within the religious worldwide very own particular tiers and intensity of strength, with the super sphere containing the high-quality energy. The depth and the character of electricity possessed with the aid of manner of every sphere, is predicated upon upon the pulsation or vibration of that sphere. It is consequently now not possible for a spirit living inside the decrease sphere, to look or experience the higher spheres of religious international. To revel in a better diploma a sprit wants to expand to the volume of power, at which a higher sphere is living.

Time, Space, electricity (The spiritual Dimensions)

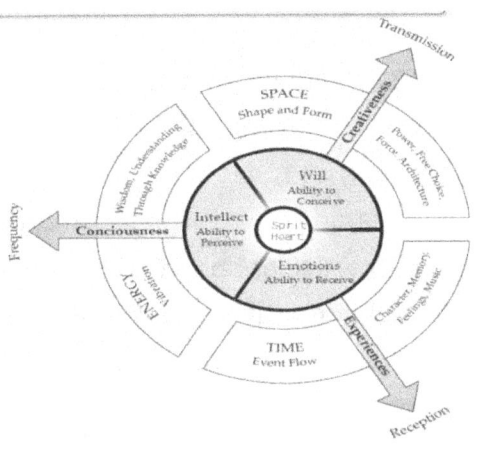

? The mystery of "Reality" in the spiritual global:

As we define the specific energy levels of spheres in the spiritual worldwide, we are able to denote that the earth is at the bottom degree of electricity as compared to the non secular worldwide, due to which, it reviews a linear location of power area and time. From the mystic literature, we're able to check the notation of "astral", which defines the middleman united states of america, among the earthly and the non secular lifestyles. It is the area which defines the mysterious creation phenomenon of each the bodily and the spiritual lifestyles paperwork.

When the spirits within the lighter sphere benefit the strength or the inner potential, they shift toward the higher spheres and may see those residing in the lower spheres. The substance located in each sphere is critical for residing in a particular sphere. So while higher sphere population visit the lower sphere, they very very own the unique substance of the decrease sphere.

The dimensions of Reality

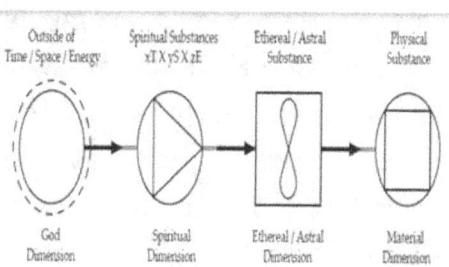

According to this layout the supernatural strength of God is beyond any period. This lifestyles is unfastened from the restrictions of area time and energy. Being on the excellent stage, all of the creatures, whether inside the non secular domain or the bodily location, are observable and controllable by means of using way of him.

The spiritual factors of region, time and strength come next within the level, wherein every sprit research a separate revel in. Based on those reviews precise spheres or tiers are created in the religious domain.

The Astral vicinity is the middleman period which comes, earlier than the bodily place of the earth.

?   The non secular global granting existence to the fabric global:

Although separated thru top notch domain names, but the interconnection some of the worlds is powerful. The loss of functionality of human mind to pursue and apprehend this truth can't make us deny this interconnection.

The bodily worldwide Patterned after the religious worldwide

Before a bodily life form passes to the religious global or earlier than a spirit takes a adventure within the direction of the earth, it passes through the astral dimension. As the material existence has the simple unit of DNA, Astral lifestyles has the four elements or forces, denoted as; air type (A), earth kind (E), water kind (W) and fireside type (F). These elements are contrary to the bodily earth, air, water and fireplace. In Astral lifestyles the earth pertains to the stress of gravity, fireplace is a representation of electromagnetic forces, water denotes the robust forces and air pertains to the inclined stress.

The mysteries of the religious and the bodily lifestyles are very a whole lot had to be mentioned so that it could pave the way inside the route of the relationship of an individual alongside together with his spirit guide.

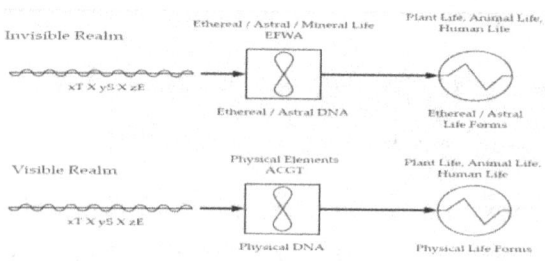

Chapter9: Communicate To Your Spirit

In the preceding sections we have were given referred to the data bearing on the spiritual global, the principle difference e the numerous worldwide of bodily and religious international. This records changed into very essential to be understood, as we are able to be discussing the connection with the spirit guide of an man or woman, in this section of the ebook. Only if you understand approximately the realities and phenomenon of the non secular global, you may make this connection better.

The questioning gadget being completed in human thoughts is a way of creating particular energy, which varies in keeping with the form of the concept being produced. This power can be transmitted to, and absorbed through using the spirits within the higher spheres, which in the end reason the relationship between a person and the spirit manual. Many human beings accept as authentic with that to be able to talk to the spirits and especially the spirit manual of an character, one want to have a separate remoted room or a constructing like a prayer hall. Although it could workout session to gain the attention, however we can't claim that connecting to the spirit courses relies upon upon such remoted region. The exceptional component favored is to create power transmission channel. Spirit guides will not communicate you back through verbal or written messages. Spirits may even deliver the feedback inside the shape of strength codes. Sometimes these messages can also take the form of symbols, mind, signs and symptoms and signs and symptoms and signs or synchronicities. The loss of objectivity in the area of non secular connections occasionally make humans annoyed approximately the interest, however it's miles the principle feature of spiritual connections,, that the whole thing is implicit however understood through the connecting ends.

? Have a agency notion:

Communicating to the spirit publications may be learnt or facilitated with the help of some zero.33 individual, but the motion depends totally on the try of the character. If you are also some of the human beings, who want to talk with the spirit guide, you want to have a organization perception at the existence of the spirit courses. When you can start with a nice questioning, the energy transmission, which is wanted for a strong connection with the spirit guide, may even very own exquisite oscillations. The conversation with the spirits, strain its manner via concentration and recognition. If you do now not believe at the life of spirits will strive to speak with spirits, you could find out the exercising dull and tiring. So in advance than any practical step, you want to keep in mind on the existence of your spirit guide. For this you could check splendid texts and literature, which speak the religious global and its realities.

? Do not allow your left thoughts conquer this verbal exchange

When you may start your workout, it's miles in a function to show up that the initial few rounds may also additionally moreover bring about a few frustration. These are the instances, whilst your left thoughts will take manipulate of your intentions and movements.

Left mind commonly governs the rational questioning and makes the moves diverted closer to the rational and logical picks. As the communique with the spirit guide may be nice nonverbal so your left mind also can bring about you to move away this illogical interest. But you want to bear in mind in the energy transmission among you and your spirit manual, with which your left thoughts can not synchronize. Once you can conquer those negating indicators out of your left mind you may get a smooth verbal exchange channel amongst you and your spirit guide.

? Set your intentions for existence

When you've got decided to speak on your spirit, it is not for fun exceptional. Spiritual publications, serve the nice reason of guiding the bodily body, in a way that the real component of existence is done. The spiritual guide isn't for telling you that which get dressed will fit you in recent times, alternatively spiritual guides are for the reason of carrying out the very great degree of strength and reality. They normally have a tendency to align your inner abilties and energies in a manner that the achievement of dreams will become much less complex and complete of extraordinary consequences. Yet the unique desires and intentions of an man or woman strain the way, wherein the mutual efforts of the man or woman and the religious guide will flow into. Once you outline a aim, the conversation and remarks turns into smoother. A smooth direction will make the development faster.

? Never omit an intuitive guidance, even inside the shape of a glimpse

Many human beings can not reap the most outcomes from the spiritual guidance, due to the truth a number of guiding indicators are disregarded or maybe misinterpreted. Getting associated with the non secular guide is straightforward, keeping the relationship and accomplishing the output is greater hard. The steerage may furthermore come within the shape of impulses or glimpses of mind, so as that you possibly can seize that electricity and act and pursue hence. Spiritual guidance lacks aim symptoms, it's far truely diffused. Otherwise in case of more obvious or tough signals, the character can also in the end come to a point of insurrection and get pissed off via the continuous knocking alerts of the spirit manual.

? Give away the misnomer that religious guide can't get to you in desires

Chapter 10: Some Common Ways of Mystic Communication with Your Spirit

The avenues via which your religious manual might also be a part of and talk with an person are unlimited. One won't get the direct interaction however the oblique techniques are on tap. Sometimes the steerage furnished through the spirit manual is inside the form of indirect clues and indicators. In this situation the appropriate interpretation of the indicators and logos is critical; in any other case a activate connection with the spirit manual is of little need.

You can connect to your spirit guide:

1.   Through the miracles of telepathy

Telepathy drives your movements, whilst you are capable of see a few thing thru the thoughts's eye. This seeing and believing may also stand up, even from a distance of heaps of kilometers. Telepathy makes it viable that the two mind centers are related in this kind of manner, that the verbal exchange is not mounted upon the physical relatedness or nearness. In case of your spirit guide, the telepathy will will will let you get the message from the manual in the form of symbols, signs, intuitions or from time to time even impulses. Telepathy particularly derives the fast burst of records or the varieties of guidance which may also require definitely sure or no form of questions. As the spirit guide is dwelling inside the spiritual worldwide, so telepathy the diverse individual and the spirit includes the relationship a number of the earthly place and the non secular place.

2.   With the help of pendulum- you could benefit miracles

In the place of religious practices, the usage of pendulum has been remarkable. Many people can also discover it awkward. Yet the underlying motive of using a pendulum for connecting to the spirits is to attain the eye. Using the pendulum is a various frame of expertise, wherein it can be discovered out to use for the religious guidance further to the recuperation way. The pendulum linked to the lengthy chain is probably moved at a constant frequency, in which each oscillation of the pendulum can result in a particular and huge meaning and sign for the character. The accurate interpretation of the message introduced via manner of manner of this technique is likewise very vital, so it's miles important that you get the steerage approximately the use of pendulum shape a few expert. Otherwise you can't get the fine benefit from its use. In not unusual exercise a pendulum chart is used with a pendulum chart. , on a bit of paper, draw a circle with eight components with "Yes" and "No" labels on top and bottom of the circle, respectively. The diagonals are categorized can be. Once you benefit the reference to the internal self, the pendulum will show you the proper course.

3.   With the "sixth revel in"

The physical existence of a frame inside the international is specifically dependent upon the use of 5 primary senses. The survival of humans is specially based upon those physical senses, which help the human beings to make correct on a daily basis alternatives. Apart from these 5 senses, which maximum of the people possess (besides with a few disability), there may be each unique duration of the texture, called the sixth enjoy. This revel in is relevant for carrying out the higher characteristic as a protracted manner because the internal and deeper self of an individual self is involved. Developing the 6th feel may also want a number of practice and remark. The keenness and attention are also the basics for the sixth experience. Pence a person learns to benefit the 6th experience, the spirit manual is an entire lot less complex to be linked.

Chapter 11: The Origin of Zodiac and the Twelve Signs

According to astrology and astronomy, the Zodiac is a circle of 12 divisions of celestial longitudes that diploma 30 levels each, which may be inside the center of the eclipse - the direction the solar makes use of at some stage in the area over a duration of twelve months. These twelve divisions had been named signs and signs and symptoms over time.

The name zodiac became firstly Greek, and it method 'a circle of animals'. This name changed into used due to the fact half of the signs and symptoms utilized in classical Greek Zodiac are represented as animals.

This is a superb representations of the symptoms and signs and symptoms of Zodiac, the symbols they were given, the longitudes and the English names that they have been accorded.

Sign	Symbol	Number	Longitude	English Name
Aries	?	1	zero°	The Ram

Taurus	?	2	30°	The Bull
Gemini	?	3	60°	The Twins
Cancer	?	four	ninety°	The Crab
Leo	?	five	a hundred and twenty°	The Lion
Virgo	?	6	100 fifty°	The Maiden
Libra	?	7	one hundred eighty°	The Scales
Scorpius	?	eight	210°	The Scorpion
Sagittarius	?	9	240°	The Centaur Archer
Capricorn	?	10	270°	The Sea Goat
Aquarius	?	eleven	300°	The Water Bearer
Pisces	?	12	330°	The Fish

These days, the time period zodiac and the twelve symptoms and signs and signs and symptoms are broadly associated with horoscopic astrology. The twelve symptoms of the current-day zodiac have their ecliptic longitudes of their first factors, and in this, zero ranges factors at Aries, it truly is idea to be the vernal equinox. This goes all of the manner to 330° which elements at Pisces.

Modern astrology is primarily based at the belief that humans have frequencies in their our bodies, emotions, thoughts and spirits that fantastically relate to the corresponding frequencies of the planet. Modern astrology is therefore geared towards exploring the connection most of the human body frequencies and the converting frequencies of the planet. This in flip is used to provide an cause for conduct, relationships and the choices that human beings make in existence. If you observe this keenly, you may look at remarkable blessings that modern astrology has on the people that accept as true with it.

The venture that many human beings face in recent times is worry to investigate what their sign says about the triumphing or the future. However, whilst you understand the many benefits these readings bring to you, it'll be smooth to triumph over the priority and always are attempting to find steering from the ones readings concerning the maximum essential elements of your existence, as an example health subjects, enterprise problems, coins topics, fulfillment in life, relationships and such lots of others.

Astrology is based mostly on a shape of era referred to as Vedic, which indicates that something is stated is proper. This may be used as a guiding component in such some of factors of humans's lives. If you are a eager follower of astrology, you could recognize that a lot this is said about the stars is right in a unmarried element or the alternative.

People should, therefore, start taking astrology and its interpretations drastically. If you haven't been doing that, get commenced out. Signs of Zodiac are pretty extremely good within the ones modern-day-day instances and those are the usage of them in case you want to make wiser selections and to overcome demanding situations that they are going via in existence.

Chapter 12: A Guide to Astrological Readings

Astrology is antique attention that has been carried over to modern lifestyles over the years. This handiest method that it's far very massive in our lives in such some of strategies, otherwise modern humans may additionally no longer problem with it masses. The current astrological readings represent our transport charts, our lives and all the planetary placements, worrying conditions, abilities, u.S.A.And downs in life and the commands that we studies every day. It is essentially the entirety that we're facing in life and what we anticipate inside the future.

Astrology is primarily based at the perception that there's a strong dating among what takes location on the outdoor worldwide and what happens inside the inner lives of humans. It is likewise based on the perception that there is a strong courting amongst what takes place up above and what takes place here on earth.

The 3 Step Guide to Get You Started

1.   Zodiac Elements

A specific chart will display the elements in 4 fundamental solar sunglasses, that is the purple, inexperienced yellow/silver and blue.

? Red – Represents Fire

Zodiac Signs - Aries, Leo, and Sagittarius.

Characteristics - Headstrong, lively, impartial, revolutionary, passionate and inspired

Rules the Body - Heart, blood, heat, photons

? Blue-Water

Zodiac Signs - Cancer, Pisces, Scorpio

Characteristics - Nurturing, Intuitive, Caring, Loving, Mothering, Emotional, Protecting

Rules the Body - Cells, Womb, Emotions, liquids

? Green - Earth

Zodiac Signs - Capricorn, Taurus, Virgo

Characteristics - Grounded, Productive, Sustaining, Nurturing, Sensual, Nature Loving

Rules the Body - Bones, Muscles, Skin

? Yellow/Silver- Air

Zodiac Signs - Gemini, Libra, Aquarius

Characteristics - Intelligent, Flighty, Inspirational, Quixotic, Fun, Communicative

Rules the Body - Mental Processing, Breath, Lungs

2. The Zodiac Signs

The Zodiac wheel is a solar 365 days, and this is how fantastic to apprehend the 12 signs and signs and signs and symptoms of Zodiac. Each of these zodiac signs and symptoms and signs and symptoms and symptoms represents a month. Seasons and nature are brought into the zodiac as a way to make it easy for people to have a look at what is taking place spherical them and indoors them, after which they may be able to recognize higher the relationship a number of the 2.

Aries is, for example, younger, raring and fiery even as Capricorn is the old earth that is enduring the merciless wintry weather. It is sluggish but pretty decided.

All the signs and symptoms and symptoms are;

- Sagittarius

- Scorpio

- Libra

- Virgo

- Leo

- Cancer

- Gemini

- Taurus

- Ares

- Pisces,

- Aquarius

- Capricorn

three. The Planets

Astrology is extra or an lousy lot less the each twelve months clock, with the 12 signs and symptoms and symptoms due to the fact the one three hundred and sixty five days and the planets because the fingers. The planets right here are the moving our bodies; they flow for the duration of the 365 days. As they go with the flow, the meet unique planets on the way and they transmit the energies of other planets onto the earth, after converting those energies via their private frequencies.

The alignments of those planets, similar to keys on a keyboard are both discordant or harmonic; they each art work with every remarkable nicely or they'll now not. This may be very giant whilst you are studying contemporary astrology. If Pluto and Saturn, for example, are discordant, we are capable of anticipate a tough courting maximum of the two. If Venus and Mars are orbiting in harmony, however, we will expect a better dating among the 2. This is how splendid to recognize the type of dating you have got with one-of-a-type people to your existence. You every get alongside aspect them, tolerate them a piece otherwise you do no longer get at the side of them the least bit.

Chapter 13: Horoscope Map

A horoscope map in real enjoy is an astrological chart that represents positions of the sun, moon, planets, certainly one of a type astrological factors and the sensitive angles at the time an occasion happened. In this detail, a horoscope map can be very massive as it represents the ones kinds of factors at the time of someone's start to be able to carry out their character. The map is made from the translation an astrologer have to have at the sun machine and it's far strictly primarily based on the place of the solar at the time of start of the man or woman in question.

In western astrology, an astrologer has to examine the best time and starting region of a ladies and men whose horoscope map he desires to draw. The nearby time is then modified immediately to famous time. The astrologer will then convert this time into the local sidereal time of start as a way to calculate the ascendant and midheaven.

The ascendant is one of the four number one angles in the horoscope, the number one residence and the most effective. It is the easternmost or sunrise aspect.

The midheaven is also an angle in horoscope, the 10th house, and the second one maximum powerful of all of the four angles.

The astrologer then consults the ephemeris, a set of tables that has a list of the area of the sun, moon and planets in a particular twelve months, date and sidereal time with the regular stars as the primary element of reference.

The difference the various Greenwich longitude and the longitude of the location in question is taken via the astrologer on the way to decide the actual community propose time on the delivery region so as to show wherein the planets is probably seen above the horizon at the ideal time and place in query. The planets that have been hidden underneath the earth can also be visible within the horoscope.

The twelve signs and symptoms of Zodiac are the symptoms and signs and symptoms which might be used in the horoscope map to represent the planets.

In order to apprehend what your horoscope method, you need to go into your beginning date, region of begin and date of delivery. The outcomes will provide you with an perception into your individual and perhaps assist you apprehend the beyond and gift higher. A lot of people use those interpretations to shape their destiny that allows you to avoid some of the demanding situations that they may face in the future.

These days, subjects had been made plenty a good deal much less complex, to the amount that you can get your horoscope interpretation on-line. Astrologers provide you with up to date horoscope maps that you can use if you need to recognize your individual higher further to the character of your companion or family member. This may additionally need that will help you plenty in knowledge your behavior and additionally inside the installed order of a better courting with distinctive human beings. Better decisions may be made once you recognize the ones objects nicely.

Horoscope Map Reading

? The sun signal gives trendy records approximately a person in reference to their beginning date, place of shipping and time of beginning. You can also get a widespread evaluation approximately a few other person when you have their transport facts. This way, you will apprehend their character higher.

? The growing sun is thought to be more huge as it offers an in-depth records about someone. This is what you want to constantly bypass for if you want to apprehend yourself better if you want to make smart alternatives for the future. You also can take a look at out the growing sun reading of each special significant individual in your existence.

? The moon sign is in addition crucial in such masses of strategies. It offers facts bearing at the emotions of a person and their intuitive factor.

Horoscope readings are very important in such an entire lot of approaches because of the reality via them, you could calculate the astrological compatibility amongst yourself and each different man or woman to your life. Use the horoscope map or the start chart software software to evaluate your findings with the findings of the opposite character you're interested in, or the affection of your life. The consequences will provide you with an in-intensity analysis about each of you and what you can assume for the future. This may be very critical in case you want to experience a happier love lifestyles.

Chapter 14: A Deeper Look at Star Signs

Star symptoms and signs and signs and symptoms are pretty big, and they may let you recognize lots of things to your life. The well-known character symptoms are derived from the 12 signs and symptoms and symptoms of Zodiac. Your start date is used to determine your famous person signal as illustrated under. If you want to recognize what your Zodiac signal represents, you want to pick out out your famous man or woman signal.

Birth Date	Star Sign
March 21- April 19	Aries
April 20 – May 20	Taurus
May 21- June 20	Gemini
June 21- July 22	Cancer
July 23- August 22	Leo
August 23 – September 22	Virgo
September 23- October 22	Libra
October 23- November 21	Scorpio

November 22- December 21 Sagittarius

December 22- January 19   Capricorn

January 20- February 18   Aquarius

February 19- March 20   Pisces

With this records, you could with out issues discover approximately your beyond, your present and moreover your destiny. You also can understand the manner you relate to excellent people to your life.

Star signs and signs and signs and symptoms are used to determine compatibility in brilliant sorts of relationships, whether or not personal, business employer or every exceptional. If you are seeking out a partner who thinks greater or a bargain less inclusive of you, and behaves the same as you, for instance, you may choose one that has the identical big name sign as you. Two Aries will, for example, assume and behave the identical. Leo or Sagittarius, instead, will make perfect companions with Aries and Gemini, or Aquarius can be close to excellent companions with Aries.

The illustration below will help you understand compatibility higher as a manner to pick out companions in lifestyles efficiently:

Star Signs well matched with Aries

Perfect Partners   Sagittarius and Leo

Almost Perfect Partners   Aquarius and Gemini

Souls   which   might   be   Likeminded Aries

Opposites that entice you   Virgo and Scorpio

Learn out of your variations   Taurus and Pisces

Not your destiny   Cancer and Capricorn

Totally Incompatible   Libra

Star Signs well matched with Taurus

Perfect Partners   Capricorn and Virgo

Almost Perfect Partners   Cancer and
Pisces

Souls   which   is   probably   Likeminded
Taurus

Opposites   that   attract   you
Sagittarius and Libra

Learn out of your differences   Gemini
and Aries

Not your future   Leo and
Aquarius

Totally Incompatible   Scorpio

Star Signs well suited with Gemini

Perfect Partners   Libra and
Aquarius

Almost Perfect Partners   Leo and
Aries

Souls   which   may   be   Likeminded
Gemini

Opposites that lure you   Capricorn
and Scorpio

Learn out of your variations   Taurus
and Cancer

Not your future   Pisces and
Virgo

Totally Incompatible   Sagittarius

Star Signs nicely matched with Cancer

Perfect Partners   Scorpio and
Pisces

Almost Perfect Partners   Virgo and
Taurus

Souls   which   may   be   Likeminded
Cancer

Opposites   that   appeal   to   you
Sagittarius and Aquarius

Learn from your variations   Gemini
and Leo

Not your destiny   Aries and Libra

Totally Incompatible   Capricorn

Star Signs nicely appropriate with Leo

Perfect Partners   Sagittarius and
Leo

Almost Perfect Partners   Libra and
Gemini

Souls which can be Likeminded   Leo

Opposites that entice you   Capricorn
and Pisces

Learn out of your versions   Virgo and
Cancer

Not your destiny   Scorpio and
Taurus

Totally Incompatible   Aquarius

Star Signs properly applicable with Virgo

Perfect Partners   Capricorn and
Taurus

Almost Perfect Partners   Cancer and
Scorpio

Souls   which   may   be   Likeminded
Virgo

Opposites that appeal to you   Aries
and Aquarius

Learn from your variations   Leo and
Libra

Not your future   Gemini and
Sagittarius

Totally Incompatible   Pisces

Star Signs well proper with Libra

Perfect Partners   Gemini and
Aquarius

Almost Perfect Partners   Leo and
Sagittarius

Souls   which   is   probably   Likeminded
Libra

Opposites that trap you   Taurus and
Pisces

Learn out of your versions   Virgo and
Scorpio

Not your future   Cancer and
Capricorn

Totally Incompatible   Aries

Star Signs well desirable with Scorpio

Perfect Partners   Cancer and Pisces

Almost Perfect Partners   Virgo and Capricorn

Souls which might be Likeminded Scorpio

Opposites that attraction to you Aries and Gemini

Learn out of your variations   Libra and Sagittarius

Not your destiny   Leo and Aquarius

Totally Incompatible   Taurus

Star Signs nicely suited with Sagittarius

Perfect Partners   Aries and Leo

Almost Perfect Partners   Aquarius and Libra

Souls which is probably Likeminded Sagittarius

Opposites that attraction to you Cancer and Taurus

Learn out of your variations Scorpio and Capricorn

Not your future Pisces and Virgo

Totally Incompatible Gemini

Star Signs well suitable with Capricorn

Perfect Partners Taurus and Virgo

Almost Perfect Partners Scorpio and Pisces

Souls which may be Likeminded Capricorn

Opposites that attract you Leo and Gemini

Learn out of your versions Sagittarius and Aquarius

Not your future   Libra and Aries

Totally Incompatible   Cancer

Star Signs compatible with Aquarius

Perfect Partners   Gemini and
Libra

Almost Perfect Partners   Aries and
Sagittarius

Souls which can be Likeminded
Aquarius

Opposites that attraction to you
Virgo and Cancer

Learn out of your variations Capricorn
and Pisces

Not your future   Scorpio and
Taurus

Totally Incompatible   Leo

Star Signs well suitable with Pisces

Perfect Partners   Cancer and
Scorpio

Almost Perfect Partners and Taurus	Capricorn
Souls which are Likeminded	Pisces
Opposites that lure you Libra	Leo and
Learn from your variations and Aries	Aquarius
Not your future Sagittarius	Gemini and
Totally Incompatible	Virgo

If you have been born on the number one day or the final day of a celeb sign, astrologists say that you had been born on a cusp. If that is the case, you could advantage greater if you can check the star sign wherein your start date falls into in addition to the famous individual signal that comes earlier than or after your celebrity sign. If for example you've got been born on 19th February, you may have the dispositions of a Pisces in addition to 3 tendencies of the Aquarius and people every should determine your person. Again, if you were born on twenty first December, you can have traits of a Sagittarius further to some dispositions of a Capricorn. It is, consequently, particular to observe each for you to understand your self higher.

These are genuinely pointers although and in the event of a bounce 365 days, it's miles endorsed for human beings born on a cusp to have their personal personal horoscopes drawn up on the way to apprehend exactly what their large name sign is.

Chapter 15: Benefits of Following Zodiac Signs, Horoscope Map & Stars

A proper kind of people those day do no longer look at the astrological readings for unique reasons. Some people do not acquire as real with in them at the same time as exclusive people are too busy with their lives that they do no longer get time to have an astrologer have a look at their celebrity sign meaning or horoscope which means. If you're on this magnificence of human beings, then you virtually need to find out a reason to do this. The blessings of following what your zodiac sign way, what your horoscope say and what your famous individual signal approach will help you get began out for the right motives.

So many humans, then again, examine the ones readings strictly because of the benefits they've got had within the beyond. Some of those blessings are:

i)   Horoscope analyzing can manual you at the same time as you're going via a tough choice relating to coins subjects, health topics, education subjects, relationship topics and such a number of extra. If as an example you want to do commercial enterprise organisation with someone whose well-known individual sign you aren't well suited with, the agency may not move nicely. A horoscope studying may additionally moreover show you about it, and this may assist you to make wiser selections. Horoscopes furthermore supply smooth readings pertaining for your destiny health, the form of choices to make pertaining to coins and investments and so on. This manner, you can make a desire on the manner to be of brilliant gain to you in the future.

ii)   You can advantage masses in dealing with a dating which you are already in or one which you are approximately to go into. If you are approximately to enter right into a private courting, for example, the alternative character's well-known individual signal will help you recognize what sort of relationship the two of you can have. You can with out hassle avoid someone whose movie star sign is incompatible to yours because of the truth because of this that the connection might not artwork anyhow. Check out their Horoscope studying, and you can recognize if they may be the type of people a good way to get proper right into a intense dating. This manner, you may be capable of avoid future issues. If you're having issues to your contemporary courting, a horoscope analyzing allow you to apprehend in which the hassle lies, and you could make a better preference that permits you to be glad in existence.

iii)   Your corporation gives and the selections which you make pertaining money is probably better if you are following Horoscope readings. If you're about to make investments your money in a positive venture, for instance, your superstar signal may also need to mention some thing about it, and this will assist you make a decision whether or no longer or now not to move on with the idea or no longer. Your horoscope studying can also guide you at the type of investments to make and ultimately, you could no longer lose your money in investments.

iv)   If you're having coins issues and also you want to make clever monetary options for the destiny, you may seek recommendation from an astrologer. An astrologer can propose you the use of your horoscope reading on what you have to do and what you want to no longer do a very good way to gain economic freedom inside the future.

v)   Horoscope readings also permit you to in subjects to do with artwork, your system, and career. You can also make higher options regarding the education of your children and their life in famous. You can use those readings to assist a family member, a friend or a person else that you're feeling desires your help in any manner.

vi)   Get to decorate your relationships with specific humans which you do not get on the facet of with the beneficial useful resource of information their personality better and treating them as constant with that. This will help you keep away from such quite a few issues in lifestyles, and your social existence is probably a top notch deal better.

vii)   Horoscope is based totally on technology, and it's been tested to paintings for the numerous human beings that strictly agree with and have a look at it. You can use it so that you can take preventive measures as a manner to be massive for your life. So many humans have averted situations that would have in any other case harm them in a single way or the opposite after consulting an astrologer. You can avoid a miserable situation for instance in case you avoided a relationship with someone whose celeb signal is incompatible with yours.

These are really popular blessings for the people that comply with and do not forget inside the cutting-edge astrology. There are every day horoscope readings that you could use in an effort to get guidance for every day of your lifestyles. You can get a monthly horoscope analyzing every begin of a month if you want to make things higher in a few unspecified time inside the future of that month. Yearly horoscope readings are also there, and they may be supposed to guide you every 12 months so as that allows you to stay a better life. There is, consequently, masses to advantage through such readings.

Online Horoscope Reading

Advancement in pc technology has made topics masses less complicated for hundreds humans in recent times. You can, for example, be able to get your horoscope and big name signal readings on-line from the net astrologers. This will prevent a brilliant deal whilst you're searching out an astrologer to observe your horoscope. There are relied on web sites that provide up to date horoscope readings that you may usually anticipate.

If you have got a thriller that you want to remedy to your life, get your horoscope studying, and you will get steerage that permits you with the intention to remedy it. If you are going through troubles in lifestyles, this is the manner to go. Your horoscope reading assist you to get an notion into the problem, and you can get an answer on a way to resolve that problem. This may be very easy these days because of the reality it may be performed on line. In many cases, these readings are loose.

Most of the types, we've on-line are in topics to do with love and dating as this is the area have been pretty some people want to make a better choice in. This can be because of the truth better relationships bring about better living and happier lives ultimately. Meet online fortune tellers in an effort to permit you to get a glimpse of what the destiny might be for you so that you will make higher selections to have a better destiny. You can take preventive measures if you do now not like what the reading says about your future and with the steerage of the fortune teller, you could avoid catastrophes in lifestyles.

There are online compatibility video video games as properly for those human beings that need to go into into happier and extra healthy relationships. If you haven't been making higher picks of companions inside the beyond, that may be a at the same time as to make a outstanding desire as a way to be satisfied. Play the game, and you'll recognize if the opportunity man or woman is honestly right for you. You can use the ones video video games too that lets in you to understand the sort of individual you need to be searching out if you aren't but right into a courting.

You can get associated with a psychic online as properly for any unique request that you may have.

Note: Make sure that the internet internet site you're the use of for your online horoscope analyzing is updated so you can get an accurate or close to accurate analyzing of your horoscope.

Chapter 16: How Spirit Guides Can Help You

Spirit courses have specific divine assignments. They can help you in masses of approaches. They can bring satisfaction into your existence in instances of melancholy. They allow you to make a valid preference. They guard you from threats and risk. They additionally assist you benefit a deeper know-how of who you genuinely are — your issues, dreams, regrets, goals, and hopes.

Spirit courses can help you in masses of techniques:

They deliver you an possibility.

In the spirit worldwide, there's no such trouble as fulfillment. If specific topics have been happening to you latterly, your spirit guide may be pulling a few strings. Spirit guides align you together together with your goals. They gift you with opportunities that will help you reap your desires. For instance, if you dream of going to Greece, your spirit manual may also moreover display you some awesome airfare or inn offers. Your manual might also additionally lead you to possibilities to help you increase money on your journey.

They shield you from harm.

The spirit publications will ship you a warning signal even as there's potential hazard. These courses defend you in plenty of techniques. Here are some real-lifestyles examples. Kate was mugged and threatened at gunpoint. But, via hook or by means of criminal, for reasons that she can't provide an purpose at the back of, she escaped unscathed. Here's every one of a kind instance, Edward changed into hiking inside the wilderness and could not discover his manner decrease lower back. Out of nowhere a mysterious stranger appeared and helped him discover his way once more to the camp. A woman named Michelle were given a robust urge to prevent her car as she approached the intersection, so she did. A 2d later, she noticed a vehicle collide with every different vehicle. If she hadn't stopped, that automobile may moreover have collided with hers.

They carry joy into your lifestyles.

When you experience down or depressed, your spirit guides can also additionally appear in unique office work to cheer you up and produce happiness to your life. They also can come in the shape of kids or lovable pets. They may additionally additionally additionally appear within the shape of joking spirits. They can also lead you to funny films or symptoms that can help lighten your day. Spirit courses assist decorate your optimism and they help you have a look at the brighter component of lifestyles.

They help you discover solutions to the most important inquiries to your life.

Spirit guides encourage you to inspect your self to find out the solutions to the most crucial questions to your lifestyles. They help you find out your fears and your life purpose. They moreover assist you understand the matters which might be important to you. So, at the same time as you're feeling misplaced or forced, it'd be a exceptional idea to call your spirit guide for assist.

They assist you analyze valuable existence instructions.

Spirit guides teach you the most important lifestyles commands. They help you observe the fee of self-love. They additionally help you research out of your errors and wreck your awful desire styles. These publications help you take a look at out of your disasters and successes. They additionally allow you to apprehend essential life instructions together with:

- It's smart to surrender poisonous friendships.

- It is k to fail.

- You do not must be precise at the entirety.

- No one is invincible.

- Live under your way.

- Talk to your loved ones as regularly as you could at the same time as they're although alive.

- Be type to yourself.

- Invest in stress-busting sports.

- When you're tired, take a step returned.

- Do no longer look at your lifestyles to others.

- Prepare after which go with the flow.

- You are the best one in fee of your happiness.

- The nice is however to return.

- It is ok to experience unhappy.

- It's adequate to make errors.

- You're particular enough.

So, when you have a "eureka 2d", your spiritual guide can be working his/her magic.

They help increase your creativity.

Some religious courses help growth your creativity. They assist you re-conceptualize the hassle. They help you brainstorm a couple of thoughts and correctly weigh the viability of every. They placed you "within the region" or "within the groove" in which you enjoy a apparently countless go together with the float of mind.

They help you do the right problem.

Your spirit guides will deliver you symptoms and messages that will help you make the right selection and do the proper issue. They keep you from developing a big mistake.

They make you experience secure and loved.

The spirit publications make you sense loved and steady, specifically at the same time as you're on my own. They come up with a hurry of protection, warm temperature, and love. They make you sense consisting of you aren't alone.

When to call your Spirit Guides

You can call your spirit guides and ask for assist at the same time as:

- You are in want of answers.

- You need help.

- You are in risk.

- You are faced with hard choices.

- You are experiencing financial problems.

- You revel in misplaced and depressed.

- You are experiencing a creator's block.

- You have a warfare with a cherished one.

- You revel in some component that's out of this world.

- You truly need a person to talk to.

- You are forced.

- You are careworn and beaten with the useful useful resource of all your duties.

You can name your spirit publications anytime and anywhere. You'll examine severa pointers and techniques to help you touch your spirit guide in a while on this ebook.

Chapter 17: Types of Spirit Guides

Not all spirit courses are the same. They have specific makes use of and reason. They have precise obligations. Here are the 14 maximum not unusual forms of spirit publications:

Joy Guides

The pleasure guides convey us pride, laughter, and happiness. These guides continuously remind us to loosen up, set free, and genuinely experience existence. These courses regularly take the shape of joking spirits, kids, and fairies. When you're stressed, worn-out, or depressed, your pleasure manual will remind you to have a study the brighter issue of factors. Your joy manual brings extra happiness and amusing into your existence. They help get rid of the negativity on your life.

Joy courses may be mischievous from time to time and they pick to play pranks. They might also additionally hide shoes and different subjects.

Protector Guides

The protector publications are guardians who guard us from risk. These courses are strong and that they have got a massive physical frame. These publications are of indigenous records. Many people agree with that protector courses typically appear inside the form of Native Americans. They can also appear as animals together with panthers, elephants, or lions. You can call upon the ones publications at the same time as you're in want of braveness, energy, and safety.

Our protector guide makes us experience secure, protected, solid, and cherished. They are liable for your safety and safety. They moreover assist you are making life-changing choices. They are calm, supportive, and mild. When you name upon your protector guide, you'd right now feel a hurry of affection, safety, and warmth for your body.

Gate Keeper Guides

Gate-keeper courses function guards of the Spirit World. They act as gatekeepers between outstanding dimensions. They provide you with get right of entry to to the numerous portals of the spirit worldwide. They furthermore help you navigate via the tremendous spirit global accurately. They'll ensure which you do now not tour too deep into the spirit global. They manual you to your journey after loss of life.

The gate keeper guides can help amplify your intuition. They let you tap into your psychic abilties, letting you enjoy non secular things like astral projection and lucid dreaming.

If you're dabbling inside the spirit global, it is crucial to work on the facet of your gate-keeper guide. Your gate-keeper will assist protect your power and deliver correct messages.

Teacher Guides

Teacher guides frequently introduce us to people every time we want a particular lesson. Our teacher guides can help us apprehend our soul agreement and the instructions that we have to examine. They help us understand our motive. They moreover make it much less complex for us to apprehend the life lesson and take the important motion. Teacher publications can supply us a hand in gaining higher know-how of the lesson and the way it pertains to our more purpose. You can name upon your teacher guide while you experience pressured in any other case you're struggling to understand your cause or path.

Creative Guides

These publications help you every time you revel in writer's block or the ravenous artist syndrome. They hold your modern juices flowing and that they encourage you to create terrific portions of art work. These publications generally help individuals who do pretty some progressive work like writers, advertising executives, dancers, artists, and musicians.

Astral Guides

Some human beings experience astral excursion. This is an out-of-frame enjoy wherein the "astral body" separates from the bodily frame. Astral projection isn't as uncommon as you located. In reality, spherical 10% of the populace claims that they have got already skilled astral projection. But, astral projection may be unstable. You may moreover bump with demons at some point of your astral adventure. Fortunately, your astral guide lets in you navigate the world even as you're doing astral projection. Your guide ensures that your astral body is going returned on your bodily frame correctly.

Reflective Guides

These guides assist you discover the solutions to deeper questions in life. They let you locate your internal troubles and remedy them. They offer you with the hazard to appearance indoors yourself so you can discover the answers in your troubles.

Karmic Guides

These guides help you remedy your collective and private karma, allowing you to step out of the wheel of karma and experience advantages, happiness, and love. These publications inspire you to apologize for the mistakes that you've completed. They moreover assist you forgive those who've finished horrible subjects to you.

Information Guides

These guides are like librarians and characteristic get admission to to Akashic statistics or the overall information. They offer you with the solutions even as desired. They regularly assist you while you're strategizing or inventing a few aspect. They also offer you with valuable facts on how the world works.

Conduit Guides

These courses offer you with a boost as you perform an intuitive act. They boom your intuition even as you're making vital selections about your enterprise, career, and specific important subjects.

Ascend Masters

These spirit guides have been human beings who have completed non secular awakening or enlightenment and that they have already ascended as angels.

Ancestors

Your deceased accomplice and kids can also act as your non secular courses. They assist guard you from chance and let you make the proper picks. Your ancestors usually pull a few strings to align you together together with your lifestyles reason.

Animal Guide

Animal publications are also referred to as totems. These publications are similar to angels, but in animal form. There are numerous styles of spirit animals, which include:

Bear – This spirit animal has been worshipped through our ancestors. They offer idea for individuals who need braveness to rise up in opposition to hard situations. This powerful guide is in contact with the cycles of nature and helps emotional and bodily recuperation. The endure permits you stand in opposition to adversity. It inspires you to do so and it improves your control competencies. It is every a healer and a teacher. The polar go through is taken into consideration as a clever trainer with the useful resource of the Siberians because of its functionality to stay on in harsh weather situations. The undergo is likewise a totem that's related to Goddess Diana and Artemis.

Butterfly – Your spirit manual may additionally come in the form of a butterfly. Butterflies constitute private transformation. When you see them often, it technique which you are moving through a special lifestyles cycle. Butterflies also signify playfulness. They help you upward thrust above earthly matters and set up robust religious connections. If you see a butterfly, it is able to imply that you need to have a look at a difficult scenario or a hassle with lightness and positivity. The appearance of a butterfly might also suggest which you want to characteristic more shade for your life and you want to loosen up. In Japanese way of life, the white butterfly symbolizes the soul of a cherished one. So, if you see a white butterfly often, your deceased loved one may be looking over you.

Coyote – The coyote symbolizes humor. It reminds you now not to take matters seriously. It symbolizes adaptability and playfulness. If you notice a coyote, it is a reminder not to take subjects too substantially. It reminds you to open yourself as much as possibilities and keep subjects easy. When you phrase an picture of a coyote, be geared up for surprises and surprising top notch occasions.

Cat – The cat is a symbol of staying power and independence. It is also a symbol of interest and healing. When you be aware a cat all the time, it's miles a signal which you want to be affected person and that you want to wait and act best while the time is proper. It permits you explore the one-of-a-kind areas of your existence.

Crow – The crow symbolizes existence magic, destiny, personal transformation, intelligence, and better mindset. This guide will assist you get in contact with the mysteries of lifestyles. It helps you to pass past your illusions. It permits you to domesticate values of willpower and fearlessness.

Frog – This spirit animal symbolizes cleaning, rebirth, renewal, abundance, and transformation. This manual allows you clean the toxic and horrible energies. People who've the frog as a totem can also moreover furthermore have the functionality to move awesome geographical areas.

Dragonfly – This totem brings delight and lightness into your life. It also symbolizes adaptability, transformation, and recognition. This spirit guide encourages you to polish and show your proper colors to every body round you. It lets in you to open up to the wonders and magic of nature. It's additionally the photo of fact. If a dragonfly indicates up abruptly for your lifestyles, you can need to glance through your illusions. It additionally manner that you want to look out for deception and study the intentions of the humans around you.

Hawk – This spirit animal is a messenger of the spirit global. It symbolizes religious cognizance and it represents the strength of observation. It permits you have got a observe the people spherical you and take movement at the same time as the time is proper. This spirit manual complements your ability to steer and lead. It pushes you to increase robust values and clairvoyant skills. It encourages you to be aware of the info in your existence. If your spirit animal is a hawk, you'll be inclined to peer visions in your goals. You'll actually have a strong instinct and extrasensory capabilities.

Horse – This spirit animal is a the use of strain that consists of you thru existence. It represents passionate desires and strong emotions. Likewise, it symbolizes your strain to reap existence and precise your actual self.

Lion – This totem symbolizes assertiveness, power, and courage. It enables increase your private power. It moreover serves as an outside energy or authority that dominates some components of your existence, being a picture of personal struggle and anger. Your lion non secular guide permits you manipulate your temper and competitive impulses. It encourages you to specific your anger in healthful strategies.

Panda – The panda is a powerful spirit animal that represents peace, moderate energy, nicely precise fortune, and a high wonderful outlook. It is extraordinarily sensitive. This totem reminds you to chase after your goals. It also reminds you to set up sturdy private obstacles. It helps you feel at ease and be steady within the worldwide. It encourages you to love and deal with yourself. It permits you to live slight and agency at the identical time. It offers you the capability to demonstrate slight strength in difficult situations.

Tiger – This spirit animal symbolizes personal energy, courage, strength of thoughts, and unpredictability. It encourages you to show courage and backbone. The totem continuously reminds you to overcome your fears. It represents your capabilities to conquer the restrictions in lifestyles.

Snake – This spirit animal may also moreover appearance scary, but it in reality symbolizes restoration. It represents transformation and lifestyles changes. This spirit guide reminds you to apply your strength accurately. It moreover conjures up you to chase after possibilities that sell personal boom and development. It enables you redesign your self to make exceptional adjustments on your life.

Sheep – This totem represents your teens. It lets you get in touch together along side your vulnerability and innocence. It encourages you to be more tolerant with yourself. It moreover teaches you to take care of your self.

Whale – This spirit manual represents recognition and emotional recuperation. It moreover symbolizes peaceful power and fortitude. It is an indication of proper fulfillment. This guide teaches you to pay attention on your inner voice and discover peace. It allows you to examine your movements, intentions, and alternatives. It permits you connect to your inner reality.

Wolf – This spirit guide is a symbol of intelligence and freedom. It moreover symbolizes lack of believe. The wolf lets in you to hook up with your instincts and instinct. It assures you that you have the thoughts strength and the capability to resolve troubles and overcome demanding conditions. It moreover reminds you to show your authentic self and don't forget your instincts.

Deer – This totem represents gentleness, sensitivity, and instinct. It moreover symbolizes the coronary coronary heart strength. This totem enables refine your psychic skills and instinct.

Dolphin – This non secular manual represents intelligence, humor, delight, and playfulness. It furthermore indicates cooperation and internal power. This spirit guide allows you boom power, fearlessness, courage, and self-self guarantee.

Hummingbird – This spirit animal symbolizes playfulness, satisfaction, independence, and resiliency. This totem allows you open your self to like. It reminds you to explicit the way you experience for your loved ones. It moreover encourages you to flow via lifestyles and lighten up your mood.

Owl – The owl symbolizes intuitive understanding and data. It helps you to to see hidden such things as auras and orbs. It gives you the potential to hook up with your inner fact and takes you past all illusions and deceit. If you be aware an owl out of nowhere or to your dream, it's a warning of a functionality hazard or chance that you want to appearance out for.

Your spirit animal generally symbolizes your person, abilties, and tendencies. It additionally symbolizes your modern thoughts-set or a undertaking. Your spirit animal strengthens your non secular expertise and instinct. It additionally gives steerage. Most people have simplest one number one spirit animal, however you may have a couple of animal publications to your lifetime.

Soul Guide

Your soul guide is your crucial manual. This guide remains with you within the direction of all your lifetimes.

Different courses permit you to in precise strategies so it is vital to the touch the right one.

Chapter 18: Signs that your Spirit Guide is Communicating with You

Did you ever revel in like a person is looking you? Did you ever feel that a spirit is round you? Do you get signs and symptoms and signs and symptoms out of nowhere? If you've skilled those objects, your spirit guide may be speakme with you. Here are the pinnacle signs and signs and symptoms and symptoms that your spirit guide is contacting you:

Ringing in a unmarried ear

When your spirit guide is around you, you may experience a ringing sensation in a single ear. This can also need to reveal up even as you sense certain feelings along with happiness, love, and compassion. You might also additionally experience this ringing sensation while you're thinking about on non secular questions. The ringing sensation can also very last for a few seconds or perhaps minutes, however it's also brief. For instance, you may be watching a information phase approximately a Japanese boy who donated his piggy monetary institution to the patients of typhoon. As you enjoy that surge of happiness and altruism, the ringing sensation begins. This is your spirit manual, telling you to hold feeling what you're feeling. Your spirit manual moreover tries to inform you to percent your blessings to others. But, of route, if the ringing sensation persists for hours, you need to appearance your doctor and are attempting to find medical advice as it can be some factor else.

A sturdy feeling which you are not on my own

If you're feeling that everyone's searching you or which you aren't by myself, you'll be right. When your spirit manual is around, you'll have a strong feeling that a person is looking you. You'll experience stable and everyday however no one around – physical as a minimum.

You'll sense like someone is supporting you

Spirit guides want to collaborate. They love to help you find topics that can be beneficial in mission a undertaking. They additionally assist take place new thoughts and answers. When you're engaged in a challenge, your spirit guide can be assisting you.

You'll stumble into mentorship opportunities

Spirit courses normally provide guidance through a mentor. So, if a number of mentoring possibilities are thrown your way, your spirit guide can be running his/her magic that will help you acquire your goals and desires.

Your spirit manual is sending you a message through telepathy

When you get keep of statistics by the use of seeing some thing in your thoughts, your spirit manual may be sending you a message. Spirit guides normally communicate with you using telepathy. Your spirit manual can also deliver you a message in the shape of photographs, letters, symbols, and phrases – or a mixture of all these items. For example, if your spirit manual thinks that it's far beneficial for you to buy a selected ebook, the call of the author and the name of the e book might also furthermore pop into your mind out of nowhere. If, as an example, your soul mate is currently in Greece, you can see photographs of Greece everywhere you pass. This may be a signal from your spirit manual, telling you to visit Greece and find your soul mate.

Your spirit guide communicates with you through your goals

Your spirit manual can also talk with you to your goals. Your spirit guide may additionally take you to a considered one of a type realm through your goals to will let you go to and talk together with your deceased cherished ones.

You'll see repeated numbers

When you notice some of that's repeated 3 or 4 instances together with 888, 333, or eleven:eleven, your religious manual may additionally virtually be sending you a message. These devices of numbers have one-of-a-type meanings.

777 – This is some of that shows up in your each day existence to deliver you comfort and safety. This quantity assures you which you're being watched and guarded via your spirit guides and guardian angels. So, while you spot this enormous range, try to get in touch along side your non secular guide through prayer or

meditation. The variety 777 is associated with proposal, introspection, and tolerance. When you see this range, your spirit manual is telling you to allow waft of control, release your fears, and find out your internal electricity.

555 – When you see this set of numbers, your spirit manual is telling you to pursue your ardour, cause, and your dreams. This huge range basically tells you to do some thing new and step from your comfort region. It is a message that you are prepared for a main lifestyles alternate. It is a caution that something big goes to appear each time quick – you could get a wonderful organisation concept or an possibility to artwork remote places.

eleven:eleven – If you keep on seeing eleven:eleven, you may revel in synchronicities in your lifestyles. The universe is aligning that will help you achieve the existence of your dreams. This photo tells you to pay hobby in your intuition and pay attention to the synchronicities round you. It reminds you to take note of the possibilities and classes for your every day existence.

222 – When you notice this series, your religious guide or angel is trying to inform you which you are at the proper music and that you have to keep going. It approach that what you're doing is congruent to the preference of the Divine. When you see this range series, your religious manual is basically telling you that you are doing a awesome manner.

333 – This angel extensive variety tells you that God is with you and helping you. It manner which you are surrounded with the useful resource of angels. The big variety 333 indicates the reality that every one matters are same and that we're all one. It additionally symbolizes the union between the soul, the body, and the thoughts. So, if you see this variety, your spirit guide is also reminding you to maintain a balance amongst your spirit, body, and thoughts.

444 – This amount collection is powerful. It method that your spirit publications are beside you and so whilst you see this big variety, it is critical to be privy to the topics round you. When you phrase the extensive range 444 all

spherical you, your spirit guides are telling you to pursue your passions and paintings tough to gain your goals.

999 – This quantity represents benevolence, non-conformism, and altruism. This range additionally represents philanthropy and humanitarianism. If you spot this massive variety, your spirit guide is reminding you to pursue your soul task and lifestyles reason. Your manual is telling you to devote it slow to serve others. This variety is also a signal that a section on your existence is about to close and which you need to prepare yourself for brand new beginnings.

888 – This big variety represents high-quality exchange. When you notice this variety, your spirit guide is telling you that true appropriate fortune is on its manner. Seeing which means which you'll need to put together for a few element appropriate in your existence, and which you must trade your conduct and your behaviors to align yourself with the first-rate alternate. This variety is also a reminder from your spirit manual to do everything on your

strength to make certain that your price range are nicely in area. When you word this quantity, it's far critical to check all of your transactions to make certain that there aren't any misused price range.

666 – This might be the maximum debatable variety. Many believe that this extensive variety is the mark of the satan or the beast. This huge variety draws doubt and fear. But, in fact, this range is neither right nor horrible. It is only a signal that your lifestyles is imperfect. It is a non secular wake-up call out of your mother or father angel. When you be aware this big range, your spirit manual is telling you to pay interest on your coronary coronary heart and no longer in your head. This great range is a name for stability. When you note the variety 666, your spirit guide is reminding you to raise your mind and cross lower back your reputation to like. You want to invite your self the following questions:

• Is my preference for fabric matters overshadowing my spiritual direction?

• Am I forgiving?

• Am I giving people the benefit of the doubt?

• What am I simply fearful of?

• What topics the most to me?

• Does it definitely matter number what others bear in thoughts me?

• Who are the three most important human beings in my existence? Am I doing my wonderful to expose them how an entire lot I love them?

• Am I making the same errors again and again once more?

Remember that the range 666 is only a sign from your spirit guide telling you to evaluate your life. Your spirit manual is honestly telling you to attention on matters that make you enjoy glad and fulfilled.

Your spirit guides will contact you in specific processes. It can be via a sign, a whole lot of, or possibly through your inner voice and instinct. So, you want to pay attention.

Chapter 19: Tips on Contacting Your Spirit Guides

You can touch your spirit guides in unique techniques, however in advance than you try this, right here are a few pointers that you have to comply with in correctly speakme along with your manual:

Raise Your Energy Vibration

Most spirit guides vibrate at a higher frequency than maximum humans. So, in advance than you attempt to contact your spirit publications and construct a strong friendship with them, it is essential to elevate your vibrational frequency with the resource of doing the following:

Practice self-love.

Practicing self-love increases your power vibrations as it lets in you permit circulate of awful emotions including blame, anger, shame, and resentment. It moreover lets in you to be at peace with your self. It allows you get in touch collectively together together with your inner self it is vital in speaking with your spirit guide.

Recite a mantra.

Reciting a mantra while matters aren't nicely right away will growth your vibrations. You can use a non-public mantra like "I am love". You can also use a few trouble encouraging like "I can do this" or "This too shall skip".

Exercise.

Exercising will increase your power vibration because it makes you satisfied, honestly. It releases endorphins on your thoughts so it makes you revel in amazing. It improves yourself-self perception and it allows alleviate pressure and anxiety.

Laugh.

If you're feeling down, watch humorous movement photos on YouTube or change some jokes collectively along with your pals. This will proper away make you experience right.

Do random acts of kindness.

Doing random acts of kindness raises your electricity vibration with the useful resource of creating you feel properly. So, try to assist an antique female pass the pressure or buy a homeless guy a heat meal. A small act of kindness can bypass a long manner and it could also align you along with your spiritual guide.

Be thankful for what you've got.

Maintaining an mind-set of gratitude will boom your vibrational frequency because it increases the quantity of your happiness. It will increase your arrogance and normal psychological health. When you sense like you're vibrating at a low frequency, prevent and depend your advantages. Think about the matters that you have to be glad approximately like your own family, pastime, home, buddies, and the cash in your financial group account.

Travel.

Traveling can help growth your electricity vibration in a number of strategies. It permits you to find out your existence purpose, it shifts your attitude, and it relieves pressure. It moreover offers you a danger to try new topics and meet new human beings.

Play a few tune.

Music robotically will increase your vibrational frequency. Thus, if you're feeling down, play a few upbeat and galvanizing tunes.

When you're vibrating at a higher frequency, it is easier as a way to contact your spirit manual. It is also much less difficult for you lure notable sports and create harmonious relationships.

Clarify your cause.

Before you touch your spirit manual, it is essential to make clear your reason. Why are you speakme to your spirit guide? Do you want solutions? Do you need help? Or do you absolutely actually need someone to speak to? Remember that unique spirit publications have tremendous duties. To ensure which you touch the right one, you want to make smooth your reason first.

Contact a selected spirit manual.

As cited in advance, specific spirit guides have exceptional features and duties. Hence, with a view to get the solution or the assist which you need, you need to contact a specific manual. If you want protection and steering, you can touch your protector manual. If you're depressed, you can touch your delight guide. If you're feeling pressured, you may touch your existence guide or instructor manual.

Use crystals and stones.

Crystals and stones can cleanse your air of thriller fields and assist you to align yourself at the side of your religious manual. In contacting your religious guide, you can use the following crystals and stones:

Amethyst – This opens up your top chakras and clears your energy pathways. It allows dispose of impatience and anxiety.

Celestine – This connects you to better realms. It lets in you to loosen up and get rid of bad thoughts.

Phenacite – It cleanses your energy area or air of secrecy. It improves your instinct and makes it simpler in case you need to achieve messages from your spirit manual.

Selenite – This stone promotes dream endure in thoughts and strengthens your spirit interactions.

Angelite – This stone enables you speak with angels. It heightens your spiritual senses.

Emerald – This super stone improves your psychic talents. It moreover protects you toward terrible energies.

Herkimer Diamond – This crystal has magical homes. It allows you sharpen your psychic abilities and it could be used for telepathy. It energizes all your chakras.

Malachite – This enhances psychic visions and it opens the coronary coronary coronary heart chakra. It additionally cleanses your aura and lets you communicate collectively along with your spirit guide.

Quartz – This stone enhances your instinct and psychic competencies. It improves your clairvoyance and has strong restoration houses.

Turquoise – This stone opens up your 1/three-eye, so it enables you to talk together together with your spirit guide.

Create a region wherein you may overtly speak for your spirit manual.

To make it less hard that lets in you to the touch your spirit manual, it's far vital to create a vicinity wherein you may talk in your spirit guide. Make extremely good that the place is quiet and free of distractions. It can be a corner on your office or bed room. Decorate that vicinity with candles and non secular figures like angels. Spray that vicinity with ylang-ylang or rose scents. These aromas sharpen your senses, making it much less difficult if you need to pay attention to your spirit guide's symptoms and symptoms and responses.

Keep an open mind.

When you're communicating together together with your spirit guide, you received't constantly like what you concentrate. So, it is important to keep an open mind. It is vital to permit move of manage and permit your self to be inclined. Be sincere and take shipping of that there are matters in lifestyles you couldn't supply an reason at the back of. Lastly, discover ways to pay attention.

Be affected individual.

Your tries to touch your spirit guide won't normally attain fulfillment, so it's far vital to be affected man or woman. You should learn how to look beforehand to answers. You need to simply accept as real with that your spirit manual will provide you with the answers and symptoms which you need at the time while you need them the maximum.

Lastly, you need to consider on your spirit guides. You can not touch your spirit publications besides you in truth accept as true with that they exist. You need to just accept as authentic together along with your spirit courses and the signs and signs and symptoms and signs and synchronicities that they arrive up with. Otherwise, it is going to be tough at the manner to touch, communicate, and construct a relationship along with your spirit manual.

Chapter 20: Contacting Your Spirit Guide
Through Prayer

Saying a prayer does no longer handiest assist you to talk with God. It additionally allows you to talk collectively together with your spirit manual or your father or mother angel. Saying a prayer permits you in masses of strategies. It offers well timed direction and it elements you closer to the proper choices. It moreover will boom yourself guarantee, disposing of tension and worry.

To contact your spirit guide via prayer, take a seat in a private and cushty region and then say your aim to touch your spirit guide. Then take a deep breath and say those prayers:

Prayer for Answers and Clarity

"I invite all my mother or father angels and spirit guides to be with me on this 2d. My existence has now not been desirable enough these days. I experience burdened and I experience that like my existence is stuck and I am getting nowhere. Angel of God, my determine angel, I wish that you could assist me discover the solutions that I were seeking out. I enjoy like I'm not going to discover the solutions by myself, so I want you to help me decide this out. I am relying on you. I am starting myself as much as you. I am looking ahead for your answers. Open my eyes so I can see in which you're maximum critical me. Awaken my ears so I can listen your voice."

Prayer for Worry, Stress, and Anxiety

"My spirit manual, my determine angel, I pray that you may release me from all my problems and anxiety. I am terrified of what the destiny holds for my own family, my career, and my rate range. I pray that you can deliver me peace. I pray that you may crush my concerns and boom my faith in you."

Prayer for Discernment

"My discern angel and my spirit manual, I pray that you may guide me in making the proper picks. I pray that you'll assist me make the proper choice. Grant me information to decide the top notch course of movement. Give me the braveness to do what's most appropriate. I will watch for your answers."

Prayer for Love

"My guardian angel and spirit guide, I pray that that you may fill my life with love and that you may lead me to my soul mate. I desire that you may assist me find out actual love. I pray that you may assist me heal my emotional wound so that I'll be ready to discover my soul mate and spend my entire existence with him/her."

Of direction, the ones prayers are truely examples. You can create your personal prayer – the kind that lets in you to talk from the coronary coronary heart.

After reciting your prayer, you may feel a divine or effective power spherical you. You might also see a imaginative and prescient or provide you with an idea. But, in case you see no symptoms and symptoms and symptoms or if you do now not experience your spirit manual's presence, be affected person and don't worry. Just be aware of your environment within the following few days as your spirit guide may additionally additionally offer you with the answers via a sign, a photograph, or via any other character.

Chapter 21: Contacting Your Spirit Guide Through Meditation

Meditation has an entire lot of advantages. It improves your popular emotional and religious well-being. It lessens stress and allows prevent despair. It will also boom yourself-popularity and self-esteem.

Meditation improves your resilience and could boom your rest, optimism, and attention. It strengthens your social connections and it improves your cognitive talents. But, aside from those extremely good blessings, meditation is also a effective manner to talk together along with your spirit manual.

To speak together with your spirit manual thru meditation, you want to conform with those steps:

•   Do a little stretching to cleanse your strength. You can do a few yoga poses or some simple stretching bodily sports.

•   Sit to your sacred region. You can take a seat down on a chair or a cushion.

• Take deep breaths and reflect onconsideration on the matters that you are grateful for.

• Hold a stone or crystal and location it close to your coronary heart.

• Then start to center yourself and be at peace with your self. Allow yourself to glide away and launch all of the anxiety from your body.

• Close your eyes and hold in thoughts that there's a gold mild round you.

• Let pass of all your terrible thoughts. Check in that you hold the tension to your body. Then, update that anxiety with deep breaths. Allow each breath to repair your frame at a mobile diploma.

• Let pass of all your mind as your aware thoughts falls asleep and your creativeness awakens.

• Start to name your spirit manual. Say some issue like "My spirit manual, I am proper here due to the fact I want your presence.

Please seem earlier than me and deliver me solutions."

•   Then, accept as proper with that you are status near a cliff overlooking a pristine river. Inhale and do not forget that it is really before sunrise. Imagine that there's a staircase in the the front of you. Take step one up. Continue to take steps up to the direction of higher reality and discovery. As to procure the top of the staircase, bear in mind a lush garden full of colourful plant life. This adorable garden is nothing like you've visible before. Walk thru the garden after which be given as real with a big palace within the center of the lawn. This is your religious home. Enter the palace and instead invite your spirit manual in. Now is the time. Your guide enters the room. Introduce yourself for your manual and ask him/her to introduce himself/herself to you. Spend as an entire lot time as you need collectively along with your guide. Ask him/her questions and take note of the solutions.

•   When the communication is finished. Thank your guide and allow him/her recognize that you're geared up to head away and pass decrease back to the bodily international.

- Take deep breaths. Count to 5 and then open your eyes.

You may additionally additionally say that this come across is purely in your mind. Well, it's far real. But, most of the time, our spirit courses talk with us thru our minds. So, do now not overthink. Instead, take out your mag and write approximately your stumble upon collectively together with your spirit manual. You can skip lower returned on your non secular home and connect with your spirit guide on every occasion you need it.

Chapter 22: Other Ways to Contact Your Spirit Guide

There are first rate strategies to contact your spirit guides. You can touch them thru way of following the ones recommendations:

Ask for a signal.

If you need answers right away, ask your spirit guide for a sign. You can say some difficulty like "Spirit guide, I ask you to assist me. I need to realise if I'm making the right preference. If you consider you studied that I am doing the right aspect. Can you please ship me a crimson rose within the day?" Of route, you could use one-of-a-kind devices as signs and signs.

Use a pendulum.

A pendulum assist you to speak together together with your better self and your spirit manual. Hold a pendulum after which ask your spirit manual "yes or no" questions. Hold it notwithstanding the truth that and do not pass it. If the pendulum moves to the proper the answer in your question is "positive". If it swings to the left, then the solution is "no".

Keep a spirit guide mag.

Write down all of the "intestine emotions" and messages which you come upon. Writing down the ones messages will help you hook up with your spirit publications and understand their messages. You also can use your spirit magazine for "automated writing". To do that, near your eyes and say a piece prayer. Then, begin writing down a few element comes for your thoughts. What you've written can be a message from your spirit guide.

Invite your spirit guide in your dream.

Before you fall asleep at night time, near your eyes and invite your spirit manual for your dream. You can say some thing like "Spirit guide, I am inviting you to reveal me who you're in my dreams. I need to get to recognize you deeply and I want to assemble a sturdy friendship with you." You also can say a few factor like "Spirit manual, I am stressed and I want solutions. I ask which you display me the solutions and solutions in my desires."

Your spirit guides are extraordinary beings that supply delight into your life. They teach you the most crucial lifestyles training and that they assist you discover the solutions for your questions. So, make it a addiction to talk with them regularly and build a sturdy connection.

Chapter 23: The Reality of the Spirit World

Is the spirit worldwide real? This one question is pretty tough to reply. People have different beliefs and critiques approximately the reality of this realm. If it's far going to be seemed in a non secular mind-set, this question ought to advantage numerous answers. All religions educate approximately the life of an all-effective being that made us all. The belief in a better being is as historic as time and this being is commonly recognized nowadays as God Almighty, Jesus Christ, Buddha and Allah among others.

As a protracted manner as religions are concerned, all of them appear to be very clean about the introduction of a spirit worldwide of their teachings. When God created the physical worldwide, he moreover created the spirit worldwide and certainly as God created the coolest and the lousy subjects inside the physical international, he additionally created the good and awful elements inside the spirit worldwide.

In mild of spiritual teachings, it's miles in addition believed that religious beings are higher than us in terms of intelligence and skills. Most human beings understand the ones entities as angels, demons, gods and goddesses of nature. We are taught that they have got supernatural powers that could either assist us or destroy us. Their international is parallel to us, however in a awesome size. Others take delivery of as real with that the spirit global is a place a protracted way and away. Still, others agree with that it co-exists with us.

It may be very natural for us humans to experience the need to speak with those beings. We are interested by a great form of courting that we're capable of installation with them. People do and use many processes to try connecting with the religious global. Prayer, meditation, rituals and spells are virtually a number of the methods that human beings use to speak with the better beings. It is in this method of verbal exchange that many human beings revel in a wonderful diploma of religious journey. As they percentage their non-public encounters, the reality of the spirit global is verified.

Yet, many are very sceptic as to the life of this global. There are many individuals who need to look, revel in and experience unexplainable things a good way to be satisfied. Science has an opposite view in this depend. Up till nowadays, no clinical proof allows lifestyles of the spirit worldwide. However, it does affirm on the lifestyles of things which may be beyond the human senses.

An example of that is the presence of different factors inside the color spectrum. We can simplest see colorings visible to the eye - ultraviolet, infrared and invisible, however they may be actual and they may be there. Another easy example is wind; we can't see the wind however we will experience it as it blows and due to the fact the timber sway with it.

Until then, the truth of the spirit international can be commonly supported through humans's religion and spirituality. Since, spirituality is a personal relationship with higher being, absolutely all people want to nurture and expand it. There are those who can decorate their non secular lives on their private, but others conflict and regularly seem to wander away. It is throughout the ones times that non secular mentors and precise religious leaders can help manual people within the course of locating enlightenment and religious growth.

Chapter 24: The Existence of Spirit Guides

There are many questions regarding the existence of the spirit guides. If they virtually are actual, how do they take area themselves to us? If they do hook up with us, what are their capabilities? The questions on their existence are countless and solutions are normally not enough to fulfill one's interest.

For a person who already believes in the spirit worldwide, the concept of having a spirit guide isn't always a farfetched idea. Many spirit believers attested that that they'd already professional encounters with their spirit manual. The stories are numerous as to how they communicated with the higher entities. However, it's miles just turning into to say that this must now not come as a marvel because of the reality this is how spirit courses are intended to hook up with human beings. They paintings with us on a one-to-one basis.

A spirit guide is a higher entity which have been assigned to us to assist us on our adventure proper proper right here within the physical global. They can watch over us even as we want safety, heal us at the same time as we're hurting or train us at the equal time as there's a few issue we need to analyze. Spirit publications do the ones forms of on the way to help us to fulfill our venture here on Earth.

Spiritual courses are particular from angels. It is thought that angels have not professional taking a human form. They are of masses higher ranges than the spirit guide. Spirit guides can also have lived as people in severa lifetimes so as that they have already won a outstanding deal knowledge approximately human existence and that they have got already advanced right into a better diploma of consciousness, which makes them capable of supporting us and guiding us in our earthly missions.

Spiritual courses can live with a person within the route of his lifetime. Others may also moreover simply seem in human beings's lives even as they may be desired the most. A man or woman also can furthermore have one or extra spirit guides. On the alternative hand, spirit publications might also furthermore have one or greater assigned people to manual.

Even if the spirit guides have numerous human beings to manual, the connection they've with every and clearly everyone is usually non-public and loving. Each courting is precise and entire of powerful energies.

Spirit guides may be entities that we turn to each time we have were given troubles in our lives, but this does not suggest that they're able to tell us everything we need to realize. They are there to help us flow into towards non secular growth and not grow to be aids for getting materials subjects. Their verbal exchange with us may be very subtle in order not to get within the manner of our very personal loose will.

The presence of spirit publications in our lives substantially is based totally upon on how we need to create a dating with them. The extra open we're to let them be part of our lives, the greater we will experience their presence and steerage. It is all up to us to connect with them and validate their lifestyles. We are not forced to establish a non-public relationship with them. They are simply there if we want to connect to them and they're really there as well even though we neglect about them.

Chapter 25: The Good and the Bad Spirits

Our elders have informed us that there are real spirits and awful spirits. There quite a few inspiring memories which have been shared with the resource of the usage of human beings who've encountered the fine spirits and there also are many tales of darkish research with awful spirits. It have to be understood that the spirit worldwide is likewise entire of all kinds of non secular beings. Some are very loving and very own excessive stage of attention. Others are very misleading and function low degree of focus.

Opening your self to the spirit international additionally calls for obligation. You want to use discernment to your communication with the spirits. This can also appear indistinct at the same time as you're truly starting to recognize the manner of connecting alongside facet your spirit guide and exclusive spiritual entities. It is usually encouraged to be in song with your self and pay interest carefully on the messages of your spirit manual.

You is probably questioning how you may if you are connecting with a excellent or awful spirit. Here are few signs and symptoms you may take a look at to help you out in your religious discernment.

What well spirits do:

•   Good spirits artwork in a clean manner and their messages are verifiable at some point or the other. You may realize quicker that matters begin to show out proper. Slowly, facts can be showed via unexpected events or unique sources.

•   Good spirits do not allow you to make sudden selections, but will permit you to artwork on things at your personal private pace and let you examine the lesson as you bypass along the manner.

•   Good spirits inspire you to do topics that will help you fulfill your challenge proper right here on Earth. They additionally enlighten you whilst subjects get tough. Therefore, in case you talk with them, the outcome may additionally need to typically make you revel in better. Your issues and difficulties might not be resolved proper there and then, however the smooth act of connecting with the pleasant spirits will make everything appear lighter.

What terrible spirits do:

•   Bad spirits do no longer talk in a clean way. Messages channelled with the useful aid of horrible spirits are chaotic and incomprehensible. These styles of verbal exchange will best make someone's thoughts greater cloudy and pressured. A man or woman may think that there isn't something he can do and in the long run turns into helpless.

•   Bad spirits need you to do subjects their way and they bring about horrible auras that any connection with them reasons a number of strain.

•   Bad spirits do now not want you live at peace. They will distract you on every occasion they get the risk and they are probable to run amok and reason you damage. A character's encounter with the terrible spirit is generally uncomfortable and unsightly.

As you keep your adventure towards religious enlightenment, you may discover more techniques to help you distinguish the various satisfactory and the terrible spirits. Just arm yourself with a robust experience of inner peace, so the horrific spirits will now not be capable of lie to you.

Chapter 26: Signs of a Spirit Guide's Presence

Spirit courses are continually round us. They seem themselves to us in lots of techniques. We may additionally moreover pay hobby them, revel in them or see them. We can be able to revel in the presence of our very very personal spirit guides or the spirit courses of others. However, we have to keep in mind that we are not constantly obliged to talk with. We have the liberty to decide on how we'd need to set up a relationship with them. We are not positive to hook up with each spirit manual we come across and spirit manual in turn do no longer pressure us to hook up with them.

Here are a few signs of a spirit manual's presence:

• You can see a awesome form of moderate or aura—Spiritual entities have mild energies round them. Some seem like exuding a few form of a vivid white moderate from internal and others seem like covered in a sparkling slight. You won't see them surely right in front of your eyes, but you may see a few thing that isn't normally visible normal. They can also waft fluidly and effortlessly and at the same time as you do see them, they'll evoke a experience of lightness in you too.

• You can listen a wonderful voice— Spiritual courses supply their messages in a telepathic way. It manner they speak to us in our mind. When they supply messages, we understand them in a understanding manner. Some people can also name the ones messages intuition, hunches or surely random mind. Others say there are voices on their heads and they mistook them as natural imagination. Worst of all, others may also additionally furthermore say they're hallucinations.

However, for others, they will actually concentrate a completely loud and first-rate voice like "save you", "shrink back" and "don't circulate". These normally occur in situations wherein spirits publications are seeking to maintain you faraway from harm and mishaps.

• You can also see them to your goals— Spirit publications are continuously there but on occasion due to the noise of the out of doors global in the path of our waking hours, we may not be able to pay interest or experience them. For this purpose, spirit courses might also talk with us in our goals. They do no longer appear on our desires to scare us, however they are there to offer us a very essential message on the way to assist us or to guide us. They can also furthermore appear vibrant or cloudy in our dreams.

• You might be conscious a everyday photograph or sign—There are instances while we experience a shape of heat on every occasion we pray for comfort. There also are times whilst we experience a familiar breeze every time we ask for steering. As we broaden deeper in our dating with our spirit guides, we're capable of learn how to pick out a positive signal that they may be with us. Whatever signal the spirit guide offers us, it's going to usually make us cushty.

• You can enjoy that there are spirits round you—You will have a lighter sort of feeling which could make you sense that there are higher entities with you. You will now not experience on my own and scared, however rather you'll experience included and empowered. You end up conscious which you are not on my own and that you have unseen allies which might be always strolling with you to help you every step of the way. The presence of the spirit manual have to generally be attractive and comforting to you.

Chapter 27: How to Connect with Spirit Guides

Accepting the idea of the life of spirit manual is one component and connecting with our spirit manual is some different aspect. For some, they do no longer need to attach due to the reality they may be scared to try it. For others, they will be genuinely now not organized for it however.

When the time comes which you are equipped and willing to installation a dating collectively with your spirit guide, you can attempt those steps:

• Open your coronary heart and soul. This method you should loose your self from restrictions of awful feelings like hate, envy and anger. Be at peace with yourself first. This will make it lots less complicated for you to pay attention your spirit courses and actively pay attention to their messages. Meditate often because it lets you have a few quiet time with yourself. This will help you prepare your soul to hook up with your spirit publications.

Set a certain time every day to really sit down down, loosen up and listen to yourself. Free your thoughts of any worldly trappings. Gradually increase your meditation time as you get comfortable doing it. Do now not be afraid with the concept that you're going to lose your self if you meditate. In reality, what takes place while you meditate is which you are honestly finding your self.

• Do now not get annoyed effortlessly. As you still supply yourself a few quiet time each day, you may be aware that your head will no longer close up. The greater you meditate, the extra chaotic your thoughts becomes. You can also pay interest your non-public voice for your head otherwise you my also assume you pay interest a person else's voice. Many thoughts will come and in the end, you might imagine you have got come to be crazy. Well, do not surrender. Eventually the mind will quiet.

• Get Personal. When the thoughts starts offevolved to be although and quiet, you could begin to talk together along with your spirit manual. Ask for the call of your spirit guide. If you recognize the choice of your spirit publications, your dating with them turns into concrete and demonstrated. The call of your spirit manual can be located out to you in a personal and loving manner. Talk to your manual as in case you are speakme to your self, however through this time, you will be conscious that it isn't yourself you are talking to.

• Establish acquire as real with. Just as our relationships right proper here on this planet goals believe, so does our courting with our spirit guides. Once you have associated together in conjunction with your spirit manual, supply your 100% take into account to him. When you ask questions, the primary idea that comes on your mind is shape of constantly the proper reply; this is similar to trusting your intestine.

• Stay Awake. This method you want to be equipped to accumulate the messages all the time. Spirit courses deliver messages on every occasion, everywhere and anywhere. Be open to synchronicities regular and you may effects observe the solutions, the steering and messages that your spirit guide is trying to talk with you. If you do now not get the message the first time, it'll be repeated to you till you will get it.

• Become friends with them. Treat spirit courses as you deal with a pal and pay attention to them as you pay attention to a pal. Be gentle to them for they are additionally mild to you. Talk to them commonly and let them live in you coronary heart.

• Never save you studying. Spirit guides will constantly assist you become a higher person. As you boom within the enlightenment of the spirit guides, you ought to be conscious that there are regardless of the fact that masses to analyze. Accepting the reality which you notwithstanding the truth that have an extended manner to move is likewise accepting that fact which you nevertheless need the assist and guidance of your spirit courses. As lengthy as you allow them to comprehend you, your spirit publications will in no way become bored with staying with you all the time.

Chapter 28: How to Work with Spirit Guides

It is pleasant to artwork with spirit guides just so your life turns into much less tough. However, there are matters which you want to do via the use of coronary heart so you should make the connection paintings in your very private best hobby. You need to remember that it takes hundreds of strive in your detail to harness the help of your spirit guide.

When you decide with spirit guides, you want to make certain whom you're working with. Remember that there are terrible spirits usually seeking out a danger to stir your inner peace and misinform you. You want to ensure inner your self that it's miles your spirit manual that you in fact are dealing with. The relationship need to be very comforting and appropriate to you. There should now not be any room for uneasiness and doubt.

Before starting to paintings with spirit publications, say a hint prayer. This will cleanse the encompassing with any terrible energies and this could prepare for a more sizeable and deeper conversation collectively along with your spirit manual. In your prayer, be precise to name high-quality your spirit guide. Be vocal at the side of your cause to connect best with the notable spirits. Your prayer will orchestrate brilliant energies in order to create an environment wherein you may effortlessly listen your spirit guide.

Here are ways to paintings with spirit guides:

• Attract them for your mind. The most effective manner to allow them to hook up with you is to think of them. Visualize them for your mind, as they arrive, take form and emerge as alive to your mind. They also can even seem to you to your physical international. Spirit publications are fairly modern. They can discover approaches to better display themselves to you. They will make sure that the encounter will continuously deliver pleasure and particular amazing emotions. The regulation of appeal works in this way; you appeal to what you found. The greater you consider your spirit publications, the more they may show themselves to you.

• Keep a journal. Writing matters down will assist you turn out to be extra aware spiritually. Jotting down notes will not first-class permit pass over subjects that you already experience, however it will furthermore remind you of factors that you need to do to be able to beautify your reference to your spirit manual. It is a truth that the human memory is confined to an quantity.

With a mag, retaining music of your improvement in non secular development could be much less complicated. In addition, writing down notes will help you positioned into block and white the messages that your spirit manual is making an attempt to impart to you. The messages can be blurry at the begin, but as you evaluation your notes, you may realize that your spirit guide is already speakme to you thru writing.

• Be everyday together along side your meditation. If there are subjects that you want to do flawlessly, you really want to exercise. This is going the same alongside aspect your motive to paintings together along with your spirit guide. By permitting your self to enter a deeper and more potent meditation, you will additionally set up a more potent connection with your spirit manual. Remember that spirit courses do their artwork gently and quietly so that you additionally want to speak with them in a pretty manner. If you aren't ordinary collectively along with your meditation, it'll be tough for you to recognition on being attentive to the messages of your spirit manual.

• Ask for steerage from religious mentors. If you watched you aren't equipped enough to start your very very very own journey with regards to operating with spirit courses, it might be useful to are trying to find help from non secular mentors. These mentors can be spiritual leaders, psychics, clairvoyants and exceptional human beings who've greater recollections with the non secular entities.

• Know what spirit courses can do. You ought to understand that spirit guides are not the agencies of cloth topics. Be aware that they'll be proper right here to offer consolation every time you are in pain and hurting. They can provide you with manual while you experience by myself and helpless. They allow you to make better alternatives on your existence specially on the subject of religious increase and studying. At times of hassle, they may provide you with safety. If there are pending risks, they will be able to come up with warnings. They will let you in restoration all sorts of pain, be it emotional, social and physical.

• Know furthermore what they can't do. Spirit publications do no longer make choices for you. They simplest enlighten you, but you need to be the satisfactory to exercise the winning of free will. Do not ask spirit guides to clear up your troubles. You can only ask guidance, but you want to resolve it yourself. They do not provide cloth topics or repair subjects in the bodily global. They do not supply lottery numbers or assist get the present day day model of a car. They aren't servants at your beak and make contact with. However, they will be usually there to walk via your element no matter what.

- Consider your spirit guides as your lifetime partner. You had decided on them and that they had decided on you. You had a settlement already to be together even in advance than you've got got been born. They introduced your spirit right right here within the world whilst you were born. They stroll with you as you live your earthly existence. When your life proper here is over, they'll convey you lower again to the opposite aspect.

Chapter 29: 10 Exercises to help you connect with your spirit guide

To find your spirit manual is an difficulty of beginning the method of connecting with them. These schooling allow you to. Try to hobby and maintain your idea on one purpose: "I choice to make touch with my Spirit Guide. »

First, prepare via making sure you may now not be disturbed.

Lesson 1 - Simple meditation

Put yourself proper proper right into a meditative kingdom and draw a photograph of your Personal Spirit Guides to remind you of the manner they appearance nowadays. Place this photograph somewhere outstanding in your mattress room, to remind you of your Spirit Guide touch.

We advocate you to make the initial contact together together along with your Guides while you are in a relaxed, relaxed usa and try to contact them, at the least numerous times each week. Often even as a person turns into upset or beneath pressure, they discover the contact hard to make. This is while you need an amazing manner to loosen up your self very well and protect your self, then reattempt touch.

Remember: whilst you're disillusioned, you separate yourself from Spirit. They do no longer separate themselves from you.

Lesson 2 - Listening and Viewing

It's time to fulfill one in every of your spirit publications.

Today you may ask spirit questions that aren't non-public, and may be answered via Yes or No.

They may be observed by means of using physical sensations to your body which consist of:

•   Pressure on top of your head - starting of the crown chakra.

•   A sensation on the left facet of the frame or face.

The left thing gets, the proper detail sends.

The left side is going to the proper factor of the thoughts, the intuitive factor.

Before you begin, you can enjoy the presence of your spirit manual.

Find a quiet place, freed from distractions. Relax and get comfortable. Clear your thoughts. Focus to your guide.

Send the concept ... Hello!

You may pay interest a greeting, but this isn't always essential.

Send your Yes or No question telepathically or verbally i.E. Is these days Monday?

Relax and permit the solution to go back really as a idea.

Continue with exceptional non-non-public Yes or No questions until you are comfortable. Keep operating closer to. There is not any hurry! Spirit has no 'time' table.

You may additionally additionally exercising this with some other manual.

Lesson 3: Getting to Know your Spirit Guide

Prepare paper and pen.

Send the message: What is your call?

If you've got hassle know-how the call, popularity, then come as near what you pay interest as you can. Spirit will take delivery of some thing call you supply. Names may be lengthy and make have to be shortened. There may be a couple of name for a spirit i.E. Spirit Eagle.

Begin a speak. Trust what you pay interest.

Send the message: (Name of guide) Are you equipped to reply questions?

Wait for an affirmative answer.

Sample questions

• Do I understand you?

• Have you ever helped me? If so, how?

• How many spirit guides do I actually have?

- What is the purpose of our connection?

- Are you my dual flame?

- What is my venture?

- Are you my only spirit manual?

- How many publications do I in reality have?

- Other

Lesson four - Other Lifetimes Together

Prepare questions. Get cushty. Greet your spirit manual.

Sample questions

- Did we understand each different in another lifetime?

- How many lifetimes have we been related? In what courting?

- Have we ever reversed guidelines wherein I even have turn out to be your spirit guide on the same time as you lived at the Earth plane?

- Have you continuously been in my life on this incarnation?

- Other

Lesson 5 - The Universe, Creation, Reality

Prepare a hard and speedy of questions relating to the Universe. Take some time over as many durations as needed.

Sample questions:

- Explain reality.

- How huge is the universe?

- How and whilst was it created?

- Is there existence on exceptional planets?

- Do entities watch us from UFO's or extraordinary places?

- Did I understand you in an alien shape?

- Are there angels?

www.ingramcontent.com/pod-product-compliance
Lightning Source LLC
Chambersburg PA
CBHW051005140626
46546CB00016B/635

PRAISE FOR THE RELUCTANT BOOK MARKETER PODCAST

Jody's effervescent, upbeat message can be a big motivator for those looking for that little "push". In one particular episode, I noted a line that is extremely important for all writers/authors/storytellers to know:

"Books are valuable to people…"

Let that sink in.

We writers can be an introverted bunch at times, and seeing past our own world and imagining the impact of our work on others is a truly remarkable thing to consider.

You can certainly write a story for yourself; for others to consume it means everything.

THOMAS MULLER

I'm a regular listener to The Reluctant Book Marketer. As a writer and a reader, I find the topics covered to extremely informative and Jody's boundless energy contagious. He's not only introduced me to things I never thought about or thought I needed to think about as a writer, but other writer's journeys, their stories and what they've done that's worked and didn't work. And even though the podcast is titled "The Reluctant Book Marketer," even if you're not in the process of marketing a book--or even writing a book--you'll find his conversations and monologues well worth your while. Check it out!

RICH HOSEK - HOST OF BEDTIME STORIES FOR INSOMNIACS

"Move over Seth Godin, it's time for Jody Sperling!" I listened to one of the short episodes but then I went back to binge consume. Jody has a great mind for book marketing. Authors, pay attention. Casual listeners also tune in for fundamentals.

JOHN MAYE - HOST OF THE BINGE WATCHERS PODCAST